T0312052

New Ways to Teach Using Cable Television

A Step-by-Step Guide

Randi Stone

CORWIN PRESS, INC.
A Sage Publications Company
Thousand Oaks, California

For information address:

Corwin Press, Inc.
A Sage Publications Company
2455 Teller Road
Thousand Oaks, California 91320
e-mail: order@corwin.sagepub.com

SAGE Publications Ltd.
6 Bonhill Street
London EC2A 4PU
United Kingdom

SAGE Publications India Pvt. Ltd.
M-32 Market
Greater Kailash I
New Delhi 110 048 India

Library of Congress Cataloging-in-Publication Data

Stone, Randi.
    New ways to teach using cable television : a step-by-step guide /
author, Randi Stone.
        p.   cm.
    ISBN 0-8039-6563-X (pbk. : acid-free paper). — ISBN 0-8039-6562-1
(cloth : acid-free paper)
    1. Television in education—United States.   2. Cable television—
United States.   I. Title.
LB1044.72.S76 1996
371.33′58—dc21   96-51273

This book is printed on acid-free paper.

97 98 99 00 01 10 9 8 7 6 5 4 3 2 1

Corwin Press Production Editor: S. Marlene Head
Editorial Assistant: Nicole Fountain
Typesetter: Rebecca Evans
Cover Designer: Marcia R. Finlayson

Contents

Preface

There is one thing stronger than all the armies in the
world, and that is an idea whose time has come.

Victor Hugo

I am a 1996 Continental Cablevision National Cable Educator
Award Winner. Thirteen educators were selected from schools
across the country. But I knew that anybody can do what I did—in
fact, when I won I was absolutely flabbergasted. I wanted to know
how many people had entered the contest. Was I selected from hundreds? Or perhaps thousands?

I discovered that 15 people from the state of Massachusetts had
entered, and I was selected from this pool. I wanted to know where
the other 985 applications were. Something was going on here: I got
the gnawing feeling that teachers weren't taking advantage of cable
television.

My award consisted of the following: a TV and VCR for my
school; a Cable in the Classroom watch and piece of luggage; a proc-
lamation from our city mayor; an all-expenses-paid, 3-day trip to
Washington, D.C.; a tour of C-SPAN and participation in the audience of C-SPAN's *Washington Journal*; an awards ceremony; meetings
with Congressional representatives; a sunset riverboat cruise on the
Potomac; and a tour of the U.S. Holocaust Memorial Museum. I was
famous for 3 days and it was one of the best experiences in my life.

I met Continental Cablevision Award winners from all over the nation. I wanted to put them all in my suitcase and take their cable stories and their invigorating energy back with me to my elementary school. I enjoyed meeting this outstanding group of educators and you will, too. Their teaching tips in Chapter 6 are inspiring.

I left Washington, D.C., with the feeling that only pockets of teachers in schools were using cable television. It was something to which some teachers gravitated, but about which others knew absolutely nothing. This had to change. Surely, teachers would use cable in their classrooms if they knew how to do it. It was so easy and very beneficial to students.

I felt as if I didn't need to take an airplane back to Boston: I could have flown *myself* fueled by a combination of excitement from the upcoming cable programming and the need to share this resource of cable television to anyone who would listen. This book is written as if you were sitting next to me on the airplane. Thanks for listening.

Purpose

This step-by-step guide encourages all teachers to add the dimension of cable television to their curriculum. This timesaving book provides you with the road map I wish I'd had throughout my teaching journey. It tells you how to find out what programming is available. It introduces you to the cable world from my perspective—that of a teacher. It gives you the information you need to begin using cable television effectively in your classroom and possibly become the next Cable Educator of the Year.

Who Should Read This Book?

New Ways to Teach Using Cable Television is for K–12 teachers, administrators, and future teachers. This how-to book cuts across grade levels and explains, in universal terms, an initiative known as Cable in the Classroom. This book will help administrators see how cable television fits into education as an effective teaching tool. It should also be used in teacher training programs to help future teachers become technologically savvy.

Description of Contents

Chapter 1: Turning On. This chapter gives you a brief background of cable television. What is cable television? What is instructional television? This is the place to find out.

Chapter 2: Getting Started and Checking Connections. Now that you know what cable television is, this chapter helps you find out if you have it and what to do if you don't. There are ways you can start using cable in your classroom today.

Chapter 3: Conquering VCR-Phobia. You can get around VCR-phobia. You don't have to be a technical wizard to take advantage of Cable in the Classroom programming.

Chapter 4: Using Cable TV Programs in the Classroom. This chapter tells you what's on cable television. Read about Project Techno-Weather, my award-winning unit in which I used The Weather Channel. This chapter gives you detailed information, including phone numbers and addresses, of a dozen cable television networks. Find out how to obtain free support materials and get started.

Chapter 5: Cable TV as a Teaching Tool. This chapter gives you suggestions to incorporate Cable in the Classroom programming into your curriculum. You will find a list of on-line addresses, classroom viewing tips, and contest and grant information.

Chapter 6: Tips From Continental Cablevision National Cable Educator Award Winners. What are other teachers doing with cable television? This is the place to find out. This group of award-winning teachers offers tips to help you get the most out of cable television.

Chapter 7: Creating an Information Renaissance. This is a transcript of the remarks made by FCC Commissioner Rachelle B. Chong at Continental Cablevision's National Educators Awards Luncheon. When I heard Commissioner Chong deliver this speech I wanted to share it with all of my colleagues at my school. This is my chance to share her inspiring speech with yet a broader audience.

My goal is to give you a path to follow and save you precious time. I hope you will find this book helpful and begin to develop your own projects. I would like to include your project ideas in a future book to share with other educators. Please send your cable television stories to Randi Stone in care of Corwin Press, Inc., 2455 Teller Rd., Thousand Oaks, CA 91320-2218 or e-mail me at RandiBeth@msn.com.

RANDI STONE
Lowell, Massachussetts

Acknowledgments

The teaching and learning taking place at the Shaughnessy Humanities School in Lowell, Massachusetts, sends lightning bolts of energy into me daily. This wouldn't happen without the outstanding leadership of our superintendent, George Tsapatsaris; Dr. Steve Arnoff, the director of educational technology; Linda Lee, our principal; and Roberta McBride, our assistant principal. Thanks to all of the students, staff, and faculty of the Shaughnessy Humanities School.

I would not have won this award without The Weather Channel. By using The Weather Channel programming in my unit, Project TechnoWeather was born. This experience opened my eyes to a world of cable programming that I didn't know existed. I am thankful to Tamra Cantore, Carolyn Jones, and Judy Dyer of The Weather Channel.

Thanks to Continental Cablevision for having the National Cable Educator Award contest. I would especially like to thank Nancy Larkin, Sandy Bosco, Mike Leone, and Sue Bennett for their never-ending encouragement and support. Taffy Patton, manager of education outreach at *Cable in the Classroom* magazine, steered me in the right direction and generously granted permission to use the following material from *Cable in the Classroom* magazine: Cable in the Classroom: Television Programmers and How to Reach Them (pp. 42-45), Classroom Viewing Tips: Suggestions for Teachers (pp. 53-54), Twelve Tips for Effective Television Use (p. 61), and Copyright Basics (pp. 61-63). I appreciate her time and energy.

Thanks also to Bryan, my VCR guru/husband, and my 3-year-old daughter, Blair, who says she wants to be a teacher when she grows up. Thanks to my mother (a retired teacher of 35 years), my father, and my brother.

I also want to thank the following outstanding teachers: my third-grade teacher, Mrs. Marilyn Smith; Dorie Docherty; Jean Goldberg; Dr. Roda Amaria; and Dr. Robert Gower.

A team of very special people helped with this book. I'd like to thank them for their time and expertise.

Susan Abbey, vice president for community affairs, Court TV, New York, New York

Kathleen Alley, media specialist, Braden River Middle School, Bradenton, Florida

Tom Baker, teacher, Moorpark High School, Moorpark, California

Betty Ballard, teacher, Independence High School, Charlotte, North Carolina

Dick Bears, president, Court TV, New York, New York

Kathy Bello, teacher, Belvoir Elementary School, Greenville, North Carolina

Richard Benz, teacher and media specialist, Wickliffe High School, Wickliffe, Ohio

Kathy Bruni, teacher, Butler Junior High School, Oak Brook, Illinois

Paul Drummond, teacher, Ealy Elementary School, West Bloomfield, Michigan

Robert Gallagher, manager of educator outreach for Discovery Networks, Rockville, Maryland

Marla Gartner, teacher, Ealy Elementary School, West Bloomfield, Michigan

Philip Geiser, language arts teacher and technology coordinator, Southern High School, Stronghurst, Illinois

Micki Hammond, teacher, Smith Valley Elementary School, Kalispell, Montana

Joseph Hoffman, teacher, West Bloomfield High School, West Bloomfield, Michigan

Mark Hotz, vice president of affiliate and consumer marketing, CNBC, Fort Lee, New Jersey

Cheryl Jensen, teacher, John F. Kennedy High School, La Palma, California

Pat Koravos, Education On-line manager, Discovery Networks, Rye, New Hampshire

Josie Levine, Discovery Networks, VCR team member, Discovery On-line educator, Flushing, New York

Lucy Levy, vice president of development, Turner Educational Services, Atlanta, Georgia

Chuck Lewis, director of media and TV studios, Manchester High School, Manchester, Connecticut

Connie Louie, educational technology coordinator, Massachusetts Department of Education, Malden, Massachusetts

Donna and Gene McCreadie, teachers, Temple City High School, Temple City, California

Manuel Moreno, teacher, Lincoln High School, Stockton, California

Jim Neary, educational access coordinator, Lowell, Massachusetts

Libby O'Connell, director of community programs, A&E Television Networks, New York, New York

Nancy O'Donnell, social studies teacher, Saint Joan of Arc Elementary School, Aberdeen, Maryland

David Oliver, teacher, Egypt Lake Elementary School, Tampa, Florida

Larry Pratt, education outreach specialist, C-SPAN, Washington, D.C.

Don Ratte, general manager, Lowell Cable Television, Lowell, Massachusetts

Dr. John Richards, general manager, Turner Educational Services, Atlanta, Georgia

Mary Rollins, senior manager of Discovery Channel Education, Bethesda, Maryland

Jay Roy, principal, Rollinsford Grade School, Rollinsford, New Hampshire

Kevin Sacerdote, teacher, Paxon College Preparatory School, Jacksonville, Florida

Pat Schneider, media consultant, Teachable Tech, Inc., Atlanta, Georgia

Matt Scott, general manager, Chelmsford Access and Information Network, Chelmsford, Massachusetts

Madlyn Steinhart, media literacy specialist, IS 43 District 21, Brooklyn, New York

Dr. Frank Watson, teacher, Plantation High School, Plantation, Florida

Sandra Welch, executive vice president, PBS Learning Services, Alexandria, Virginia

Joanne Wheeler, manager of education and marketing services, C-SPAN, Washington, D.C.

Gaylen Whited, broadcast sales and acquisitions specialist, GPN, Lincoln, Nebraska

Micheline Woolfolk, library media specialist, John M. Gandy Elementary School, Ashland, Virginia

About the Author

Randi Stone is the computer teacher at the Shaughnessy Humanities School in Lowell, Massachusetts. She is a recipient of the Continental Cablevision National Cable Educator Award.

A graduate of Clark University, Boston University, and Salem State College, Ms. Stone holds credentials for elementary education, and a master of science in broadcast communication. She is currently working on her doctorate in education at the University of Massachusetts, Lowell.

Introduction

One afternoon last spring I met Jim, our new school district television director. He found me in the computer lab between classes, and started telling me about cable television programming. During our conversation, my mind raced. This sounded wonderful! Who'd have known that I would soon end up using cable in my own classroom and win a national contest honoring me as a 1996 Continental Cablevision National Cable Educator of the Year?

As we spoke, I grew more and more excited as I considered the possibilities. I am the computer teacher at the Shaughnessy Humanities School in Lowell, Massachusetts. I teach children in Grades 1–4 how to use technology as a tool. I try to position the computer lab as an extension of all of the other classrooms.

The Shaughnessy Humanities School has approximately 540 students. We have a computer lab with 25 Macintosh computers and classroom computers on an AppleShare network. My desk is in the computer lab, which I call my classroom.

I was thrilled to find out that our computer lab was already equipped with all the necessary hardware to connect us to our local cable television provider. My classroom was connected to the world! I wasn't exactly sure what this meant for my students. I had been using a TV and VCR in the computer lab to play videotapes for the past 2 years. I once tried to change the channels on the TV, but didn't get a picture so I assumed I couldn't receive television stations. Certainly, I assumed, if teachers had been doing more with TVs, I would have known.

I ran up and down our school corridors poking my head into classrooms asking teachers if they knew anything about cable television and its educational programming. Some people said they had heard something about it a few years ago. Others said they didn't know what on earth I was talking about. When I turned to my assistant principal, Roberta McBride, she actually knew some things about it and encouraged me to dig deeper.

Jim had taken the TV and VCR cart and wheeled it over to the front of the classroom where the cable outlet was located. He told me every classroom in our school had such an outlet. My jaw dropped. This wasn't so—he couldn't be right. As he plugged in just one cable, I was red with embarrassment.

He talked about programs featuring news reports that were geared toward children so they could stay up to date on current events. He mentioned live weather reports and science shows. Could I use The Weather Channel to teach children about the weather? My mouth watered and my heart raced. This was unbelievable. Had my head been in the sand all this time?

So I subscribed to *Cable in the Classroom* magazine, an outstanding resource for educators, and couldn't wait to receive my first issue. I turned to the yellow pages in my telephone book and found my local cable access telephone number. At the time I didn't even know how to program a VCR, but I knew at least one person in our school who did. I was determined to find the educational programming Jim described.

The winter of 1995 was rife with more than a half dozen snow days. I spent one entire snow day reading and rereading *Cable in the Classroom* magazine. I highlighted it, dog-eared the pages, took notes, and compared it with the listing of cable television networks that I got in my home. I felt like a little kid in a candy store.

I had questions, so I called my local cable company and found Sue Bennett, the program director and executive producer of *NewsCenter 6* for Continental Cablevision and my Cable in the Classroom representative. Sue took the time to answer my questions and never once made me feel as if I had just arrived on Earth from a distant planet.

Next, I turned to the free support materials listed in *Cable in the Classroom* magazine. I headed for the telephone and called away. I called every number listed. Sometimes I talked to live people, but on some days I'd leave messages on one answering machine after another. If there wasn't a phone number, I wrote letters requesting materials to the addresses listed.

Soon after, every day became a holiday. My mailbox at school overflowed with information from CNN, Court TV, and the History Channel, to name but a few. Faxes started pouring in. This was better than Disneyland to me. The more I read, the more it seemed as if every school in the country was involved in this except us.

I didn't yet know how to use a VCR to record a show, but I planned to figure it out so that I could finally get my hands on the educational programming about which I was reading. It's funny, because I am tremendously comfortable around computers. Just ask me to install software, troubleshoot network problems for an entire school, or fix a printer—I seem to do it effortlessly and by rote. Programming a VCR, on the other hand, was something new for me.

I decided to do what teachers in our school do when they have computer questions. They ask for help—so that's what *I* did. I asked for help and got it. Our school music teacher, Kevin Reilly, along with my husband, Bryan, got me started. I gave my husband lists of programs that were relevant to my lessons and in one month, Voila! I had a tape library to supplement my classroom curriculum. This innovative up-to-the-minute cable television programming can add a new dimension to teaching literally overnight.

So I got hooked on cable television—but I felt alone. How come other teachers weren't salivating over these materials? Jim had said that cable television was catching on. But perhaps it was happening slowly. Certainly, too slowly for me.

I think back to the significance of that one meeting. He catapulted me into a new way of thinking about the way I teach. He showed me I had the tools already and basically just pointed me in the right direction and set me free. Now I would like to take the opportunity to do for you what Jim did for me.

It is no secret that VCR-phobia is running rampant. There are jokes about it. We all have a VCR yet it seems hardly anyone knows how to use it. Across the country, VCRs in homes blink "12:00" and have been sitting this way for months, if not years. The same is true for VCRs in many schools. In many classrooms across the United States, VCRs are sitting either unused or underused.

I'll never forget presenting my contest-winning cable project to our school district principals at a meeting. I began my presentation by showing a videotape of children participating in the project. I was rewinding the tape when an administrator approached me with a look of awe in his eyes. I thought he was about to commend my efforts with the children. Instead, pointing to the VCR, he jested, "Wow, you know how to use that thing!"

You can do exactly what I did. As a teacher, the journey is definitely worth it. My commitment to integrating cable television into my classroom has led me to a treasure trove of programming that will enhance my everyday teaching experiences, my life, and my students' lives.

Turning On

The History of Cable Television at a Glance

Cable television channels have broadcasted educational programming since the early 1980s. During this time, there were strict educational copyright guidelines whereby one could only use a particular program in the classroom within 7 days of the taping, after which one had to discard it. One really couldn't use the programming for general viewing because it violated copyright provisions.

In the late 1980s, Chris Whittle introduced Channel 1, which provided schools with an advertiser-supported daily newscast. Whittle also provided schools with a satellite dish to receive the newscast, along with TVs and VCRs. This raised a series of ethical issues with regard to advertising in the classroom.

When Channel 1 was introduced, Ted Turner—former owner of CNN, the world's largest news-gathering agency—decided to develop a daily noncommercial educational newscast for schools. He rallied the support of others in the cable industry, encouraging the cable systems to deliver this programming to schools over the cable wire and working with cable programming networks such as the Discovery Channel, A&E Network, and The Weather Channel to consider producing noncommercial programming for schools.

An extended copyright window was set up for such Cable in the Classroom programming. The cable industry for the very first time decided to package educational programming for schools and brand it as the industry's commitment to education. That is how the national Cable in the Classroom organization was born. A group of leaders from the cable industry, including Continental Cablevision's Amos B. Hostetter Jr., got together and founded it as a nonprofit organization to foster the industry's commitment to education.

What Is Cable in the Classroom?

Cable in the Classroom is a public-service initiative of the cable television industry. It is a joint project of local cable operators and national cable programmers to provide schools with free basic cable service and more than 525 hours of commercial-free educational television programming each month. For more information, call (800) 743-5355.

About 84% of students nationwide (more than 40 million) have access to Cable in the Classroom in more than 75,000 schools. More than 8,500 local cable companies and 32 cable programmers together have invested over $420 million in America's schools since 1989 (more than $80 million during the 1994–1995 school year alone).

What Cable in the Classroom Is Not

Cable in the Classroom is not a commercial, profit-making venture. There are no costs, contracts, or viewing requirements imposed on schools; and all programming is commercial-free. Cable in the Classroom is not meant for passive "homeroom" viewing. Teachers use as much or as little of the programming as they wish, integrated with classroom discussion and exercises, to fit their own lesson plans.

What Is Instructional Television?

For more than 30 years, there has existed curriculum-correlated material directed at teachers. State departments of education and district-level personnel know about its availability. The best way to find out about what kind of instructional programming is available in your area is to get in touch with those at the district level who are curriculum specialists. Ask if there are any broadcasts or videos available that correspond to your curriculum. You may even ask within your own school and find out that other teachers have been using it for years.

Another place to check is with your state's department of education or department of public instruction. Ask if they are using instructional television. Chances are they are using some it in some form and purchasing it on a city- or statewide basis.

I called the Massachusetts Department of Education and spoke to Connie Louie, the educational technology coordinator. She told me about instructional programming provided by the state of Massachusetts to schools during the school year. She also told me about MCET, the Massachusetts Corporation of Educational Television. Apparently, program guides are sent to school libraries across the state. So make that phone call and see what is available in your state to supplement your curriculum.

Getting Started and Checking Connections

Cable television has to be wired for your school. One can't just plug a television into the wall, turn it on, and expect to have cable programming. So the first thing to do is check to see if the building has cable access. You may find, as I did, that the facility is cable-ready even though you don't know it. You may also find that your school is planning to get cable access in the near future.

Even if your school doesn't have cable access, you can take advantage of cable television programming in your classroom by taping shows at home and showing them at school. Copyright restrictions do apply to educational programming, and these are described in Chapter 5.

How to Find Out If You Have Access

Do I have cable access in my classroom? A question like this can get lost in a school department's bureaucratic maze. Don't waste your time searching around your classroom for something that looks like a cable plug.

Call your local cable company and ask for a cable television representative. Usually they work in the local programming department and should be able to help you. Most cable companies will send a service technician to your school and your classroom to check if you have access.

A technician will be able to tell you where the cable feed begins, where it comes into the school, and where it ends. Does it end in the main office? Does it end in the library or the auditorium? Is there a drop in every room? Cable companies in most franchise agreements provide this voluntary service to various school districts. In Lowell, Massachusetts, they provide free cable drops.

How to Get Access

As a teacher, it is important to involve administration in this process so that you are all working together as a team to bring cable into the school. Also, you don't want to pursue cable access on your own only to find out that others are already working on it and you didn't know about it.

The first thing to do is to call the cable company. There are a lot of different cable companies nationwide, and each has a franchise in the area in which they service. If you aren't sure which cable company services your area, call the Cable in the Classroom organization at (800) 743-5355.

Cable company technicians are the ones who will install the cable. They have maps showing where cables already are installed. If the building has been wired, there is a good chance that all that is necessary is dropping a cable line into the school.

In most cases, cable television is a free service to schools. Cable companies are willing to accommodate schools as long as the cable is somewhere near the school and there is no huge cost involved in getting the cable to the school building.

Jumping the Funding Hurdle

I spoke with Nancy Larkin, vice president of community relations at Continental Cablevision, about what teachers could do if they don't see any funding coming their way for TVs and VCRs. She told me of some creative ways to get money for equipment.

For example, she mentioned a librarian who organized a candy bar fundraiser to buy equipment. When she got her TV and VCR, she started using the program *CNN Newsroom* and shows broadcast on the Discovery Channel, and she promoted the positive response to her principal and school board. A year later the school put five TVs and VCRs in the budget and eventually all of the classrooms had them.

Apparently, the PTA buys more VCRs than does any other organization. Nancy recommends checking with your local cable company about video equipment because it may offer equipment at a discount. This could enable you to buy perhaps twice as many TVs and VCRs.

Teachers as Public Relations Agents

Nancy Larkin said that if there were one thing she would like to teach teachers, it would be how to be public relations agents. She recommends spending 80% of one's time doing the project and 20% of one's time talking about it. The idea is to spend enough time promoting what we do so that funding for any necessary equipment becomes available. Start small and turn to your cable representative for assistance. Ask about discounts and enhancements from organizations such as the PTA.

Making Parent Connections

Nancy Larkin helped introduce the Cable in the Classroom venture to her own child's elementary school years ago. She approached her daughter's teacher and asked to help her use video in the classroom. Together they created a parent packet that was basically a form asking parents to volunteer to videotape programs for 1 week.

By doing this, the parents were participating in their children's education. The teacher followed up with a thank-you note in which she noted how the cable programming was used in class. In most cases, parents ended up watching the show and began to see the value of what technology does in the classroom. This firsthand experience on the part of parents helps when talking about the value of TVs and VCRs to the school board or PTA.

You'll want to come up with other creative ways to involve parents without burdening them. For instance, in Florida a teacher taped the cable television program *In the Company of Whales*, then sent it to students' homes with a stuffed whale in a bag along with an evaluation form. The students' assignment was to watch the tape with their parents and then complete an evaluation form together.

Whenever possible, provide opportunities for students to present what they are doing in school. For example, when a teacher heads a class project, schedule a special presentation before the school board committee. Invite your students and their parents. There is a good chance that this could be televised on a local cable channel—so consider this a great public relations opportunity.

One exemplary project, Suit Up for the Space Shuttle, involved kids creating space suits and going to space camp. An award-winning teacher set up a speaker's bureau of kids and sent notes to local community organizations such as the Rotary Club and the Lion's Club asking for an opportunity to visit and explain their class project. This was one way of getting the word out.

3

Conquering VCR-Phobia

Most people have TVs and VCRs at home. Although some instruction manuals can seem a bit complicated, most users can figure out how to record if they want to tape a show badly enough.

Once you've established your cable access, it's time to conquer VCR-phobia. It doesn't have to stand in the way of the many benefits of incorporating cable programs into your teaching. And you don't have to do this by yourself. Today many schools have library media specialists with library assistants or volunteers.

Do what I did. I found the VCR gurus (my school music teacher and my husband) and asked them for help. My husband was very surprised with my sudden interest in our VCR. I never really noticed it before. I used it to only to play *The Lion King, Snow White,* and other assorted Disney movies in my toddler's collection.

I studied *Cable in the Classroom* magazine. It listed programs that sparked my curiosity—programs that I could incorporate into my teaching as well as my own ongoing education. Sometimes I'd ask my husband to program the VCR, and as he would peruse the titles in which I was interested he would actually ask me to wait to watch them so that we could watch together. For me this affirmed that someone not directly involved in my teaching found the cable programming compelling.

Eventually, you will probably want to learn how to record shows for yourself, but it will all happen in due time. When the VCR gurus are not readily available and you need something yesterday, you will learn. In some cases, videotapes of cable programs are available to purchase. This can be convenient—but over time can be somewhat cost-prohibitive.

I don't have an actual videocassette recorder in my classroom: I have a video player that does not record. I did discover, however, that there *are* a few genuine VCRs in the school. The nearest is in what we call our literacy center. Because I didn't want to constantly interrupt our literacy teacher, I decided to do my recording at home and interrupt my husband instead.

But self-reliance—not dependence on others—is the goal of this book. As your first step toward conquering VCR-phobia, you must ask for the instruction manual. All VCRs are not the same, but they all come with operating instructions. I can remember a huddle of teachers gathered around a VCR reading directions. Our teamwork proved to be successful, and eventually we actually were able to broadcast a television program!

We were broadcasting a prerecorded television program. Programming a VCR to record a program at a future time—and in your absence—requires slightly more attention. Some surveys say less than one third of the people who own VCRs actually know how to program them to record a TV show that will air while they are away from home.

However, if you can use your microwave oven, you can definitely learn how to tape a program. And of course, once you have done it a couple of times, it will feel like you have been doing it forever, and you will do it automatically. I wish I could give you a cookbook recipe with steps to program your VCR. That would certainly simplify things. But I can't do this because all VCRs are not alike. Let me try to explain why.

Each brand of VCR was designed by a different company and there is no standardization. Each comes with its own unique instruction manual. Even automobiles are more standardized than VCRs— if you can drive a Honda Accord, you can probably drive a Ford Taurus. A helicopter pilot, on the other hand, probably could not fly an F-14 Tomcat. VCRs are like helicopters and Tomcats. Knowing how to program a Sony VCR does not mean you will know how to program a Mitsubishi, or vice versa.

Ten Tips to Conquer VCR-Phobia

1. *If at first you don't succeed, try reading the instructions.* Keep original instruction manuals in a safe, centralized place. This includes manuals for the television set connected to the VCR, the camcorder, and the VCR itself. Every new VCR comes with an instruction booklet.

The instruction manual eventually will prove helpful. Look at the manual and try to figure out the directions. Even if you are still having difficulty getting the VCR to work right, at least you've explored the manual enough so you can ask the appropriate questions.

2. *Call your local cable company.* I never thought cable company personnel would be willing to take time out of their day to talk to a classroom teacher about how to operate a VCR—but I was wrong. Local cable companies, as a customer-service function, do this regularly.

3. *Find out who purchased the television and VCR and ask where the person bought it.* This could be the library media specialist or principal. In principle, all good dealers want to generate future business and therefore should be willing to help their existing customers.

4. *Students, especially of junior high and high school age, usually can be helpful with programming a VCR.*

5. *If there is a remote control, keep it handy at all times.* Keep extra batteries available.

6. *Chain a set of directions to the VCR and cart.*

7. *Be certain that both the cable box and the television are set to the proper channels.*

8. *Don't unplug the VCR.* Keep it plugged in so that its clock remains accurate. If you do have to move it, reset the clock immediately.

9. *If you haven't purchased equipment yet or you are looking to buy new equipment, consider a combination TV–VCR, which is generally easier to use than component TV and VCR models.* (But be forewarned: A number of people have said that although the combination TV–VCR is easier to handle, if one breaks, they both have to be sent out for repair.)

10. *You could also look into VCR Plus+®.* This is a handheld remote into which you program the code numbers for any given show from your *TV Guide* or local television listings. Once set, the VCR Plus+® will automatically turn on your cable box and VCR at the right time to record a show in your absence—and even turn them off

when it's done! It can even record multiple television shows at different times on different channels. Some brand-new VCRs have built in VCR Plus+®.

Tips From a Formerly Videophobic Educator

Kathy Bruni, a language arts teacher at Butler Junior High School in Oak Brook, Illinois, is a Continental Cablevision Educator Award winner. She told me how she overcame her videophobia.

Kathy has Murphy's Law posted in her classroom: Anything that can go wrong will go wrong. When Kathy first started using cable television, she was flustered by the equipment. She considered her situation ridiculous because her 11-year-old students could program the VCR and she couldn't. Ultimately she became too embarrassed to keep calling her colleague down the hall to come to her rescue, and so she put together teams of students in each of her classes to help her.

She also made large, bold, step-by-step directions, which she laminated and chained to the equipment carts. She says once you've got the system down (which may require some trial-and-error in the beginning) the eventual payback is unbelievable. Her trick is to have the directions readily available in every single place where she may need them. The idea is to simplify, simplify, simplify—and it took her a while to get to this point. Kathy's directions contain four steps.

How to Record a Cable Television Program

1. Make sure all of your power connectors are on—this means check the cables and connections, and check that your power is on.
2. Make sure you have a clean tape and that the tab is not removed. Make sure your tape is inserted into the machine.
3. Double-check your program times in your local directory against your cable guide.
4. Set the timer a little ahead to give lead time (you may record the tail end of another program, but you won't miss a key moment in the beginning of the one you want).

Finding the Cable Signal

One excellent question to ask is, Where does the cable signal come into the school? I remember one day when I had about 30 pairs of children's eyes staring at me waiting to watch The Weather Channel. I confidently turned on the TV and then paled as I stared into a soap opera. What happened? Where did The Weather Channel go? I hadn't touched anything.

This is how I learned there was a main cable switching box in our school that somehow regulated what I could watch in my classroom. I also learned that sometimes channel settings can be lost and TVs must be reset to the appropriate stations. When The Weather Channel mysteriously disappeared that afternoon, I realized I didn't have total control of the TV and VCR setup in my classroom.

Most schools do not have TVs and VCRs in every classroom because of insufficient funding. My school, however, is fortunate enough to have a cable drop in every classroom, meaning that every classroom is at least wired. This does not mean, however, that our teachers can choose programs on cable channels at any time without leaving the classroom. All of the teachers have to physically walk over to our main cable converter box located in a first-floor audiovisual room.

Even if the cable company is sending a cable signal to the school, that signal does not necessarily go to all of the classrooms. It might just stop in the library, meaning that only the library has cable access. Therefore, it's important to identify exactly how the cable signal comes into your school.

Matt Scott, general manager of Chelmsford Access and Information Network in Chelmsford, Massachusetts, recommends designating a department to be in charge of recording programs. Chelmsford teachers fill out a cable television request form listing the programs they would like to use in class. The videotape is dropped off at the school. This way, teachers don't have to change the channel or do their own recording.

If you are a teacher planning to get cable access, be sure to try to get the cable signal as close to your classroom as possible. The best way to do it is probably also the most costly. You want to have a TV, VCR, and a wire run directly to your classroom along with a converter box. This is the way you do it at home. It should be as easy to get a cable signal into your classroom as it is into your living room.

Using Cable TV Programs in the Classroom

What's on cable television? Everything. Turn to *Cable in the Classroom* magazine and call every network and channel and put your name on their mailing lists for support materials. In addition to what is available for free, there are products and services that you can get for a fee. For example, you can get videotapes, software, and Internet connectivity. Ask for information about network products and services.

There are hundreds of networks offering educational programming to teachers, and I could write a separate book on each one of them. I have selected a dozen networks, and at the end of this section I have compiled an expanded list with telephone numbers and addresses.

I also refer to award-winning projects. Many educators have developed innovative projects that earned national attention for themselves, their schools, and their students. By reading how they put it all together, you may get some ideas about how a particular cable television network can work for you.

The Weather Channel

During my winning trip to Washington, D.C., I attended a breakfast meeting sponsored by The Weather Channel. This was a meeting

I will never forget because it was there that I was awarded a nearly foot-high glass sculpture for my creative use of The Weather Channel.

I want to start out by saying that I am no meteorologist. Teachers are not expected to be meteorologists. But there are many tools available to help teachers use The Weather Channel with their students.

The weather affects the lives and plans of each of us. We can't go out a single day without knowing the weather. I won my Continental Cablevision Cable Educator Award for Project TechnoWeather, a unit using The Weather Channel live with my students. The Weather Channel gives up-to-the-second weather reports. I was able to use the channel and integrate lessons for Grades 1–4. In this unit, part of the challenge was to ensure that all of my students were involved in writing projects appropriate for their grade level.

Project TechnoWeather

The best way for me to give you a feeling for Project TechnoWeather is to share the speech that I read to our district administration the day I was awarded the TV and VCR for my school as part of the Continental Cablevision Cable Educator of the Year Award.

Project TechnoWeather is a weather unit combining technology with cable television. The unit promotes literacy, computer skills, and self-esteem. I'd like to take you into this unit.

Picture fourth graders watching The Weather Channel, writing weather reports on computers, and then taking turns videotaping each other as would-be meteorologists. Feel the pride I felt as I crouched in the sidelines watching the students help each other use the video camera and read weather reports.

Picture a group of third graders with big smiles, singing about rain into a computer microphone while making a multimedia presentation.

Imagine how excited you would be at 7 years old hearing your voice over the school intercom reading the weather report. You would probably never forget the warm applause from your friends and teacher when you returned to your classroom. Feel the butterflies the children told me they felt.

Lastly, think how would you feel if you were 10 years old, watching a meteorologist on cable television, and then having the opportunity to meet two future meteorologists in person.

Meteorology students from the University of Massachusetts at Lowell literally awed the students. At the end of their presentation, children filed out of the computer lab, shaking hands with our guests. Step into my heart as I watched the students' faces beam.

Winning Lesson Plans

METEOROLOGISTS LOOK OUT!

Time: Three 45-minute class periods.

Grade: 3 or 4.

Objective: The goal of this lesson is to teach children how to write a weather report and build self-esteem by providing an on-camera opportunity to report the weather just as a meteorologist would.

Materials: The Weather Channel, computers, word-processing software, a video camera, and videotape.

Background: Because children are fascinated with television, teachers can capitalize on this by building writing assignments around it.

Procedure: First, students watch The Weather Channel and are asked to pay close attention to vocabulary and sentence structure. Children watch the mannerisms of the meteorologists. How do they say their words? Are they looking at the camera? Do they sound excited or do they speak in monotones? Using word-processing software, students write one weather report as a class under the direction of the teacher. The teacher reads the report as a meteorologist. The students write their own weather reports and print them. Using cooperative learning, students take turns reading their reports to one another.

The second class period entails final editing, printing, and reciting of weather reports, which are then videotaped outdoors. In the third and final class period, children watch the finished videotape and review themselves.

Conclusion: Children love seeing themselves on television. The lesson capitalizes on this and simultaneously promotes reading, writing, and building self-esteem.

SPRING FLOWERS WAKE UP!

Time: Preactivity—One 45-minute class period. Activity—One 45-minute class period (or more) to complete.

Grade: 1, 2, 3, or 4.

Objective: The goal of this lesson is to teach children how weather plays a role in planting.

Materials: Preactivity—flower bulbs, shovel. Activity—The Weather Channel, computers, word-processing software, and colorful flower and seed catalogs.

Background: The Shaughnessy Humanities School is a recipient of a 1995 Kids Growing with Dutch Bulbs award. We received 250 Dutch flower bulbs from the Mail Order Association of Nurseries in recognition of hands-on gardening programs for children.

Procedure: Students plant the bulbs in the fall and wait for them to bloom in the spring. Children watch The Weather Channel to monitor the weather and learn how to care for their flowers. This lends itself to word-processing activities and bookmaking. Books can be beautifully decorated with pictures of colorful flowers from seed catalogs. Another possible tie-in is a visit from the Horticultural Society to provide schoolyard ecology lessons.

Conclusion: By using The Weather Channel as a resource, children learn how flowers are affected by weather. This hands-on experience will stay with children. They plant their flowers, watch them grow, and write about the process.

WEATHER IN THE UNITED STATES

Time: Routine 15-minute lesson.

Grade: 1, 2, 3, and 4.

Objective: This is an excellent way of teaching children about the states, directions, and weather patterns.

Materials: A taped segment of The Weather Channel showing a weather map of the United States, computers, and word-processing and illustration software.

Background: The Weather Channel provides a variety of maps of the United States. By taping a short segment, children have fun learning about the states, directions, and basic map reading.

Procedure: Students watch The Weather Channel and answer the following kinds of questions: What is this state? What does the green mean? What does blue represent? Which way is north? The teacher uses this map as an excellent teaching tool and the children are excited about using television in this lesson.

Conclusion: Children participate in an ongoing geography lesson that increases their map skills and knowledge base. The Weather Channel is an extremely helpful tool for complementing geography lessons.

WEATHER REPORT IN SCHOOL ANNOUNCEMENTS

Time: One 15-minute block of time.

Grade: 3 or 4.

Objective: The goal of this lesson is to increase student writing skills and use The Weather Channel as a tool for learning. This is an excellent self-esteem–building exercise.

Materials: The Weather Channel, a computer, word-processing software, and a public address system or alternate way to communicate a weather report to the school.

Background: Public speaking is a top fear for many adults. This lesson provides an opportunity for children to practice public speaking by reading a weather report over the school intercom.

Procedure: A student or group of students watch The Weather Channel in the morning and write a weather report. When other announcements are read or at another convenient time, the student reads the weather report over the school public address system. It is important to have the student mention his or her name in the report so that teachers and fellow students can commend the student (e.g., "This is Robert Williams reporting"). This can be done daily on a rotating basis for students.

Conclusion: The Weather Channel is viewed by students as a reliable way to find out the weather. When students read their writing over the public address system, it builds self-esteem.

METEOROLOGISTS IN TRAINING!

Time: One hour-long class period.

Grade: 3 or 4.

Objective: The goal of this lesson is to introduce The Weather Channel to students and give them a first opportunity to be on camera.

Materials: The Weather Channel, computers, word-processing software, a video camera, and videotape.

Background: Feeling comfortable in front of a camera takes practice. This exercise shows children that meteorologists don't just get up one day and read the weather on television. There is training involved. By doing it themselves, children begin to see the skills necessary for reporting.

Procedure: Students watch The Weather Channel and write one weather report as a class under the direction of the teacher. The teacher shows the children how to use a video camera by explaining everything as he or she does it. The teacher shows the children a tripod and how to insert the tape into the video camera. As a group, children read the weather report from a printed copy, return to the computer lab, watch their videotape, and write about their experience.

Conclusion: Children begin to see there is more to television reporting than meets the eye. Do children look at the camera? Can the viewing audience understand the words? Were the children nervous? This lesson is a good beginning exercise to which we will return when the children are more seasoned. We will see student progress on videotape.

How Did Students Like Project TechnoWeather?

I thought that Project TechnoWeather was the best. We did so many cool things like predict the weather. We had two meteorologists come in, and we went outside a lot, too. Sometimes Mrs. Stone is really funny and she does stuff no other teacher would do! She really got us into the weather and made us do hard work but she made it fun, too! I'd do this again any time!

—*Michael*

We learned about weather. We watched The Weather Channel. We predicted the weather. Mrs. Stone taped us and let us read the weather. She put us into our own weather channel.

—*Connie*

I learned a lot of good things in computer class. I learned about the weather. Two meteorologists came to talk to us. When we were done watching the tornado on television, we went to the door and shook the meteorologists' hands while Mrs. Stone took pictures.

—*Brian*

MEET TEACHERS USING THE WEATHER CHANNEL

The best way to get ideas on using The Weather Channel is to read about what other teachers are doing.

Micki Hammond, Teacher, Smith Valley Elementary School, Kalispell, Montana. When the curriculum in Micki's school changed, she had to teach weather to fourth graders for the first time. She didn't have any books or materials on the weather, so she turned to The Weather Channel.

She began to tape 10-minute segments from *The Weather Classroom*, which are listed in *Cable in the Classroom* magazine. Her entire weather unit basically consisted of using The Weather Channel. She familiarized herself with the programming and used the vocabulary at the beginning. That first year sparked ideas for future years.

The next year, Micki and her students spent a lot of time looking at clouds. She used The Weather Channel and its *Weather Classroom* segments as jumping-off points for her cloud formation and water-cycle unit. She used Weather Channel support materials such as cloud formation charts and *The Weather Classroom Workbook*. She tailored the secondary-level lessons in the workbook to accommodate her fourth graders.

Students researched scientific facts about clouds. They also researched folklore. Did you know farmers and sailors use cloud formations to predict the weather? Students created group presentations on their sky findings. After considerable practice, the students used the video camera to videotape one another's presentations.

Micki took her students outside whenever she could. On any given Montana morning, the students could see almost every type of cloud, which they had learned to identify using weather charts. It got to the point that when Micki's students went out to lunch and left the school building, they would identify clouds.

Micki took the video camera home and taped different kinds of clouds. This turned into her assessment tool. She used it as a whole-class assessment and said it also would be easy to do this as an individual test. By superimposing a number on the videotaped clouds, the kids could be asked to write down as much information as they could about each cloud formation.

Micki, who has 17 years of teaching experience, instructs her students about weather and also helps other teachers use The Weather

Channel in their own classrooms. She does workshops across the country for The Weather Channel. I asked her to share her expertise.

Randi Stone: What advice do you have for teachers who are considering using The Weather Channel with their students?

Micki Hammond: The best suggestion I have is to keep an open mind and to look at the possibilities. Don't be intimidated about the weather because you feel you don't know enough about it to teach it. The neat thing about the weather is that it's constantly happening. It's right there.

Teachers think that in order to use The Weather Channel, they have to really, really use it. But they don't. They have to taste it first. Nobody goes into a new food, eating the whole plate right off. You taste if first to see if you like it. I latched on. I got a shovel when it came to this kind of media and started shoveling in.

Randi: How do you come up with ideas?

Micki: I get a lot of my ideas from my kids. One of my students likes to tune into The Weather Channel on-line to find out what the weather will be in the afternoon. If you let the kids watch, if there is a happening somewhere, like blizzards in Montana, just let them watch that newscast on The Weather Channel, and they will give you ideas.

Randi: Is The Weather Channel appropriate for primary and secondary students?

Micki: You can teach cloud formations on different levels. First graders can look at clouds and get the basics, such as a cirrus or cumulus cloud. You can take it all the way up to high school level, which is what *The Weather Classroom Workbook* is about. It's a higher-level book, but I adapted it for fourth-grade use. . . . That's the wonderful thing about weather. In the first and second grade, you can watch it, write about it, and use it in poetry or stories. Primary stories have all kinds of weather in them. There are many legends based around weather. You have rain gods in every culture. It's very easy to incorporate on any level. I don't think you have to be real knowledgeable in order to bring it into your classroom.

Randi: What has watching The Weather Channel done for your students?

Micki: They watch TV with a different interest level now. When we watch *The Weather Classroom*, it's a short 10-minute blurb that usually turns into a 45-minute lesson for me. Then we go back and watch it again and one comment from one of my kids was, "Wow Ms. H., it was only 10 minutes and it took us 45 minutes to get through the information that was given!"

Randi: Can you share some teaching ideas?

Micki: I usually watch a piece a couple of times before I show it to the kids. I stop it and go back. We do what's called double-column note taking. You write a question such as: What kind of cloud formation is that? Then in the second column, you answer the question. So we would pause the videotape and come up with the question, and then we would rewind and answer the question. The kids are involved not only in getting the information but also in setting up questions which can then turn out to be their test questions.

Randi: I am teaching a fourth-grade unit on the United States. How would you incorporate the weather into it?

Micki: Every day, you can watch the weather and get the update on each state or region. You can also go on-line to The Weather Channel Web site. You click to the state that you want and in that state there are major cities. You click and the actual temperature, humidity, and wind speed of that moment will come up. You can do graphing and plot the temperatures of the different states.

Randi: How do you incorporate the weather with language arts activities?

Micki: Every time you look out the window you have a poem because there is weather happening out there. You can ask your students: What are all the nouns you can think of? What are all the adjectives that come to mind? From there you can use those words to write a poem. It can be anything as simple as a haiku. You can make up your own formations. You can look out the window and look up in the clouds. If it's windy, or snowing, or raining, or about to, you can talk about the feel of the air and why it's feeling that way. . . . If you have a rainstorm or snow-storm approaching, take the students outside and let them stand in it for a second or two. Then go in and brainstorm all your nouns, adjectives, verbs, and adverbs. You will get a lot more because it's a tactile experience for them.

Kathleen Alley, Media Specialist, Braden River Middle School, Bradenton, Florida. When Kathleen opened a new school, there wasn't any money to develop an audiovisual collection. She found resources that were timely and free: Cable in the Classroom educational programming. Kathleen has won the A&E National Teacher Award, Time-Warner Cable's Crystal Apple Award, and many others. She is an educational consultant for The Weather Channel.

In addition to running the school library, Kathleen teaches television production and multimedia as a media specialist. Because the severe weather conditions in Florida are a major part of people's lives, she feels students need to know how to prepare for weather-related catastrophes as well as learn general information about weather. Therefore, Kathleen believes it is very important for teachers to provide weather education to students in an appropriate way—a way that is motivating and interesting to them, that gets the point across, and helps them realize how they can be prepared personally and help their families be prepared. Since contacting emergency management personnel in her county, she has begun to serve as a liaison between emergency management and her school.

Kathleen has worked with dropouts and potential dropouts, and has observed that at-risk students are very motivated by the use of television. By adding projects such as creating weather forecasts for the news program or having students research weather by watching The Weather Channel, the students are increasingly engaged. She used The Weather Channel to reach out to kids and give them something that would genuinely make them interested in getting to school.

Her students created multimedia projects on hurricanes, blizzards, and cloud formations. One presentation described the difference between hurricane watches and warnings. Students scanned pictures and retrieved relevant materials from CD-ROMs. Kathleen found her students coming to school early, staying late, and visiting the library at lunchtime. Her upcoming plan is to adapt these kinds of weather projects for elementary school students.

I asked Kathleen for some encouraging words for teachers. She said:

> Teachers are afraid of losing control and think television is going to take teaching from them. Nothing could be further from the truth.
>
> The most important thing is to pick and choose those things that will put your point across. You don't have to show anything in its entirety and you never should. You should show the things that are going to support or enhance the things that you're trying to teach.

Chuck Lewis, Director of Media and TV Studios, Manchester High School, Manchester, Connecticut. Chuck Lewis and his students don't do ordinary things in his video communications class. For instance, they recently worked together as a team to produce a documentary for The Weather Channel. His students got firsthand experience by being involved in a production for a national cable company.

The documentary was for a Sky Awareness project incorporating sky activities into everyday regular classroom lessons. One student actually traveled to San Francisco and acted as Chuck's production assistant. Another student acted as an on-air talent and was launched in a hot-air balloon. Other students were involved behind the scenes and on camera. Chuck wishes he'd had this kind of exposure when he had been in high school.

His students produce a monthly news show for the local community. They produce a local weather forecast using Weather Channel maps. The forecast is modeled after that on The Weather Channel, but with students instead of professional meteorologists. The students edit this show together. Chuck goes through hours and hours of diligent rehearsal with his class.

They learn about weather forecasting and how to be comfortable in front of a camera. Chuck is proud of the way his students deliver the weather forecast. They stand with maps and motion behind them and use local radar they get from The Weather Channel.

I asked Chuck to share some Weather Channel project ideas. He suggested the following:

1. Keep a language arts weather journal. Bring your kids outside and ask them to look up at the sky and make journal entries. They

can write during quiet time and have their own space to do this. Read poems relating to the sky and have them write their own. Take the kids outside and have them lie down on a nice sunny day and look up at the sky. Encourage them to use their imaginations: They may see an elephant or turtle moving across the sky with the clouds!

2. Turn off the sound and tape a weather forecast. Arrange the students in small groups and let them decode the same exact segment of the videotape. Then ask them to go in front of the classroom with a TV and VCR and, remote in hand, use the pause button and present a weather forecast.

3. Keep a local weather journal in which you track the highs, lows, and wind speed. You have an electronic weather station built right into your classroom. For the elementary school setting, this is perfect. For first graders, you can talk about how you are going to dress the following day.

4. The class can create a thunderstorm. Students can all tap their desks to emulate the pitter-patter of rain. Then they can start hitting their knees. Then someone can flash the lights. You can even listen to music and describe something up in the sky.

5. You can follow the path of the sun. Take the kids outside and draw their shadows on cement with chalk. Then come out a half hour later and see how the shadows have moved. Talk about the path of the sun. You can incorporate math.

Tom Baker, Teacher, Moorpark High School, Moorpark, California. Tom makes his math classes come alive with The Weather Channel. Every few minutes, The Weather Channel provides data on temperature, pressure, and humidity, painting a picture of where you live. His students work with that data, graph it, manipulate it, and make sense of it. Instead of treating it as nothing but numbers, they build pictures out of it and make forecasts.

I asked Tom to describe how he teaches with The Weather Channel.

I take my laser pointer and video. Then I stop, start, think, talk, demonstrate, and do it again. It's ongoing. You can take a 22-minute video and make it last for an entire hour. In one class, we talked about earthquake aftershocks. I would start, stop, then we would demo, describe, ask questions, and bounce back and forth. This is a way to reach just about every child.

Pat Schneider, Media Consultant, Teachable Tech, Inc., Atlanta, Georgia. Teachable Tech is a group of educational consultants, who all have teaching experience, that formed 10 years ago. Pat links video technology with computer technology and writes guides to help teachers use video in their classrooms. Pat acts as a liaison with The Weather Channel.

She makes sure the curriculum material that her company creates always has connections to many different media. She doesn't usually write guides asking questions about what students just saw. She creates guides asking students to think about what they just saw, analyze it, and go find other material to support what they just learned.

Pat gives training seminars and workshops. She told me support is the key for teachers to get involved with cable. Teachers must become partners with their media specialist and ask the specialist, "What is available to me?" If a media specialist says, "I don't know," a teacher has to ask where to go to find out. *Cable in the Classroom* magazine is an excellent resource.

There has to be a support system in the school, wherein teams of people, let's say a media specialist and a teacher, attend workshops together. If strong administrative support is demonstrated, use of cable will catch on in the school.

Pat worked with The Weather Channel to create a resource guide for a Look Up! project for students in Grades 3 through 6. The concept was to integrate curriculum as you pique children's interests by having them look up in the sky. They can excel in everything from language arts and visual arts to the sciences and math.

I asked Pat, who has been involved with video for a decade, for advice on teaching with cable television.

> This kind of video that people are putting out now doesn't teach. It helps kids learn. It is very different from the videos with words flashing on the screen and students writing them down because they knew the vocabulary would be on the test.
>
> We have to encourage kids to question and analyze what they've seen so that they don't fall asleep while they're watching. What do you do when you turn on some programs on television? You slump. You don't have to think about anything. You can be entertained and you can relax. But if you are watching a political speech, you can't slump. You have to really listen.

If you are expecting kids to gather information from video, then you have to spark them. You have to make sure they're focused on what they're watching. They have to look for something as they watch and apply something after they watch. The support materials come in handy. They tell you how to prepare kids to watch it, what they are going to look for, and what to do afterwards.

WEATHER WISDOM

Teachers have a tendency to sit kids down to watch an hour-long program without stopping. You can take that 1-hour program and make it into a week-long project if you break it up. You can skip parts and fast-forward through segments.

Don't turn on the VCR and walk away.

Never turn the lights off.

—Micki Hammond, Teacher,
Smith Valley Elementary School, Kalispell, Montana

The 10-minute clips from *The Weather Classroom* are a springboard to get into a class activity. You can tape the whole series on one single tape and have all of this information ready for your use.

Use the pause button to make video more interactive along the way. Always preview the program, the same way you would review a textbook before giving it to your students.

Use segments of a program. Don't just put it in the VCR and play it straight through.

We have to empower the students. Let them help us take them down the path that they want to go. They're not afraid of it.

—Chuck Lewis, Director of Media and TV Studios,
Manchester High School, Manchester, Connecticut

Cable in the Classroom is a winner. Stop, start, think, talk, and demonstrate. I am a Weather Channel junkie. I watch The Weather Channel daily because it gives me an idea of what is happening everywhere all at one time. I watch The Weather Channel because it is always changing.

—Tom Baker, Teacher,
Moorpark High School, Moorpark, California

A media specialist told me this tip and I share it all the time. Tell people about upcoming cable programs on the back of school bathroom stall doors. She gets more input from these notices than from anything else she does.

Support materials are an absolute necessity. You need something to help you bounce ideas. You just don't have the time to come up with super things all of the time for every one of the pieces that are coming out on all of the networks.

You have to do these three things when using video in your classroom:

1. Prepare the kids to watch. Spark their interest.
2. Have kids look for something as they watch.
3. Have them apply their new knowledge afterwards.

—Pat Schneider, Media Consultant,
Teachable Tech, Inc., Atlanta, Georgia

There is a wonderful little device on the front of any television. It is called the on-and-off button, and it can help you stay in control of whatever happens on that screen.

Of the things you teach regarding weather, some you just cannot show in a two-dimensional way. You have to go to that 3-D type of experience with kids. One of the best ways to do that is to provide them with television. My students in Florida would never know what it is like to be in a snowstorm because they've never been in snow. The only place that they've ever seen it is on television.

—Kathleen Alley, Media Specialist,
Braden River Middle School, Bradenton, Florida

The Weather Channel's Cable in the Classroom programming is listed under the earth sciences section in *Cable in the Classroom* magazine. The 10-minute *Weather Classroom* segments are designed to provide a practical, hands-on approach to teaching weather concepts.

For schedules with descriptions and news about upcoming programs and materials, call (800) 471-5544. Ask about The Weather Channel's quarterly education newsletter. You can write to

Education Services
The Weather Channel
2600 Cumberland Parkway, Atlanta, GA 30339

C-SPAN

Joanne Wheeler, manager of education and marketing services, calls C-SPAN a way of making the process of government come alive for children. Seeing a White House press conference on television makes it very tangible for students.

The letters in C-SPAN stand for the Cable Satellite Public Affairs Network. C-SPAN programming is commercial-free and brings public affairs, decision making, and the U.S. House and Senate directly to students. The U.S. cable television industry created C-SPAN in 1979 as a public service.

C-SPAN shows live coverage of Congressional hearings, White House Press briefings, National Press Club speeches, insights into the U.S. Supreme Court, international events and legislatures, and live viewer call-ins with journalists and public policymakers.

Educators can join the network's free membership support service—C-SPAN in the Classroom. What is in it for you? You will receive teaching guides, timely information about grants, and programming alerts. Did you know, for example, that there is a C-SPAN schedule hotline available 24 hours a day to find out what is going to be on and when? The telephone number is (202) 628-2205.

Also, you don't want to miss the C-SPAN School Bus. C-SPAN has two school buses that are mobile television production facilities and media demonstration centers. They travel across the country to demonstrate to teachers and students how C-SPAN's programming can be used in the classroom. Call your local cable company to arrange for the bus to visit your school.

Usually when people think of C-SPAN, they think it is just for high school students. This is not the case. When elementary school teachers want to show their first graders the president or the White House, the Supreme Court or the U.S. Capitol, they can show C-SPAN clips, all copyright-cleared for the classroom.

During my Continental Cablevision trip to Washington, D.C., I had the opportunity to be a member of the audience of C-SPAN's program, *The Washington Journal*. My name was drawn from a hat to ask former Vice President Dan Quayle a question. I'll never forget being televised and saying hello to all of the teachers and students back at the Shaughnessy Humanities School.

It is simple to become a C-SPAN in the Classroom member. There is a one-page application on which you provide basic information including your name, school, and current involvement with C-SPAN. It is fine if you have never watched it. Call C-SPAN at (202) 737-3220 to enroll. For further information you can write to C-SPAN in the Classroom, 400 North Capitol Street NW, Suite 650, Washington, DC 20001.

The following educators are winners of C-SPAN in the Classroom Equipment Grants. They have won TVs and VCRs for their schools. These teachers are using C-SPAN programming in their elementary as well as high school classrooms.

Kathy Bello, Teacher, Belvoir Elementary School, Greenville, North Carolina. Kathy Bello is a second-grade teacher who won a TV and VCR for her school. When Kathy read in her school bulletin about the C-SPAN in the Classroom Equipment Grant, she decided to apply because there was only one TV and VCR for three grades. Some teachers were even bringing their own home TVs and VCRs to the classroom, which to Kathy seemed like too much trouble.

Even though her school library is wired with cable, she chose to record C-SPAN at home and bring the videotape to school. She teamed with another second-grade teacher and designed a project called Choosing a President, wherein students experienced the campaign process firsthand. Children participated in debating, voting, and campaigning. They watched C-SPAN coverage of presidential debates and the results of the primaries. The other second-grade class did the same project simultaneously.

The students watched the C-SPAN debates for about 20 minutes and then came up with a definition for *debate.* They discussed the ways in which each candidate was trying to convince eligible voters that he or she was the best.

Then the students actually ran for office in class primaries and assumed the last name of a candidate (e.g., Karen "Clinton"). The classes learned about how a candidate builds a platform and wins votes. Students built platforms on the issues of homework, recess, gum chewing, and soda.

The students had their own debate wherein the candidates discussed those different topics. The rest of the class acted as reporters and compiled a set of questions for the candidates. Kathy videotaped this student debate and held another debate between the two second-grade classes. They all watched the video together.

After the debates, the students voted and elected the president of the class. She even said the class would follow the platform of the candidate. The students chose the candidate whose platform was No Homework, No Recess. Kathy thought it was important for the kids to understand how one's voting has consequences. The children didn't want to miss recess, even though that was what they voted for. There was some campaigning and they wanted to vote again.

Tip: *Encourage teachers to work together.*

Nancy O'Donnell, Social Studies Teacher, Saint Joan of Arc Elementary School, Aberdeen, Maryland. Nancy used C-SPAN as a resource to discuss the major issues on her students' minds. These included homelessness, school violence, and violence in the streets. She invited a dozen guest speakers—all people running for office. The students asked each of the candidates the same question and began to realize that the issues were of great importance, as were the elected officials who address those issues on the city, state, and national levels.

Nancy has been using cable television in her classroom for 7 years. She receives the educator guides from the Discovery Channel, PBS, and the Learning Channel. She says she is a C-SPAN junkie during the summer months. She always has a videotape in her machine ready to go just in case something comes up. She says she has at least 65 tapes so far.

Tip: *Know what is going to air. Be ready.*

Philip Geiser, Language Arts Teacher and Technology Coordinator, Southern High School, Stronghurst, Illinois. Philip Geiser won a C-SPAN in the Classroom Equipment Grant and was a national grand-prize winner even though his high school doesn't have the network on its cable system. He taped C-SPAN coverage from home during the primary elections.

Philip uses different kinds of media to maximize the benefits of his students' writing assignments. For instance, he uses a scanner to scan images and a multimedia computer to capture images from a VCR or camcorder. For one project, he had students do issue-oriented research and write candidate reports that included biographical data and candidates' stands on current topics.

The students watched C-SPAN and found images of candidates to illustrate their reports, which were captured and saved on disk. Then they placed them into their reports and used software to sharpen the images. Finally, the students printed their writing assignments on a color laser printer. According to Philip, it was the impressive output that helped him win the contest.

Philip submitted the reports as written by the students—spelling errors and all. He feels the C-SPAN representatives who presented the award recognized that this was genuine student response.

> Tip: *Experiment, and don't be disappointed if things don't turn out perfectly.*

CNN

You can begin using *CNN Newsroom/CNN Worldview* in your classroom for free. All you have to do is call the toll-free hotline at (800) 344-6219 for enrollment information. This is an unrestricted, 30-minute commercial-free news and features program developed especially for school use. The first half highlights current news topics with the top story of the day. The second half highlights global news stories covered by CNN's 20 international bureaus.

There is a guide available with a program rundown with running times, background information, questions and concepts for discussion, classroom and homework activities, and cross-curricular suggestions. Once you enroll your school as a *CNN Newsroom* member, you receive a free subscription to *T3 Magazine.* The three T's are television, technology, and teaching. The magazine showcases all CNN programming from Turner Broadcasting that may be appropriate for school use.

John Richards, general manager of Turner Educational Services, said that *CNN Newsroom* brings the news into the classroom as a focus for discussion and interaction. He sees it bridging the gap between students and their parents so that they can talk about the news and what is going on in the world.

Turner Educational Services also offers electronic field trips. These are planned educational adventures that combine live telecasts, computer and on-line technologies, and comprehensive guides to create exciting, curriculum-integrated learning experiences. You can call (800) 639-7797 for more information. These electronic field trips are not free: One trip is $299 (subject to change), and there are reduced fees for signing up for more than one trip.

Betty Ballard, a high school international studies teacher at Independence High School in Charlotte, North Carolina, taught junior high for 16 years and has been teaching high school for 9 years. She is on the national faculty for Turner Educational Services. Betty uses Turner Adventure Learning electronic field trips in her class. The last one she participated in was called Rockets on Wheels. First, you need a television and a cable feed or satellite. Then you have to call your cable company and check to see if your school is set up to receive the signal so you can participate. If you have a telephone with an outside line, there is an 800 number you can call with questions. You often get the opportunity to ask questions of the people who are doing the live field trip, right there on TV.

Betty is a proponent of electronic field trips because of the live interactive learning. Her students spoke with two race car drivers, Jeff Gordon and Steve Grissom, live from the Charlotte Motor Speedway. They were asked, "How do you keep the car on the track?" and "What is the difference between a race car and a regular car?"

This field trip had a physics focus, but Betty said you can use it for language arts, reading, history, math, science, or just about any topic. You can ask if a particular field trip is appropriate for your grade level. Call (800) 639-7797 and ask for further electronic field trip information. For enrollment and general *CNN Newsroom* information, call (800) 344-6219 or write to Turner Educational Services, 105 Terry Drive, Suite 120, Newtown, PA 18940.

CNBC

CNBC is a 24-hour cable television network that offers business information, money programming, and financial news. There are talk shows with viewer call-in segments. This is a resource for both adults and students—many people find themselves intimidated by and less than knowledgeable about the whole money process. Where can you go to find out about managing dollars, retirement funds, and college tuition? CNBC is a place to learn.

I requested support materials, and one of the items I received was a *Money and Banking for Students* lesson book that can be tailored to accommodate all students from elementary school through high school. I also received a small *Investing ABCs Terminology* manual.

Mark Hotz, vice president of affiliate and consumer marketing at CNBC, says that learning about money is not only for the super-sophisticated. The layperson, he says, hears about what is going on in the business world and thinks that those who have anything to do with it are geniuses. Mark suggests that all that is required to understand basic business and financial principles is to take a few moments *every day* to learn.

Some of the programming for classroom use includes *Smart Living*, which provides students with information that will help them become wiser consumers, and *The Money Club*, which is a half-hour program targeting personal finance and economics for younger students. Segments include a profile on Young Americans Bank in Denver, a bank exclusively for children.

The time to teach children about money, according to Mark Hotz, is now. When his 5-year-old daughter asks questions about money, he doesn't make the assumption that because she is so young, she is incapable of digesting information. For instance, when his daughter asked why movies are $5 and not $10, he explained in a way she could understand. He recommends explaining about money to children rather than answering with the typical response, "That's all they charge."

For more information, call (201) 585-6469 or write to CNBC, 2200 Fletcher Avenue, Fort Lee, NJ 07024.

Discovery Channel

The Discovery Channel offers documentaries for children. Mary Rollins, senior manager of Discovery Channel Education, says nonfiction has always been and will always will be the strength of Discovery Channel programming.

Discovery Networks sends out an educator guide that provides program descriptions, taping and copyright information, and support materials. All you have to do is call (800) 321-1832 for a free subscription. The educator guide is sent free of charge to teachers each year at the end of August and December. This 30-page, two-color booklet is an excellent resource to help you use Discovery Channel with your students.

Assignment Discovery airs Monday through Friday from 9:00 A.M. to 10:00 A.M. (ET/PT). This documentary-style program covers science and technology on Monday, social studies and history on Tuesday, natural science on Wednesday, arts and humanities on Thursday, and contemporary issues on Friday. There are video-support curriculum tools to help you use it. There are suggested readings, vocabulary words, and preview questions with answers at the end of the documentary.

For more information, call (800) 321-1832 or write to the Discovery Channel, 7700 Wisconsin Avenue, Bethesda, MD 20814.

The Learning Channel (TLC)

When you take the best from the Discovery Channel library and package it for younger viewers, you get *TLC Elementary School*. Because the attention span of younger viewers tends to be shorter, *TLC Elementary School* offers short 3-minute clips on everything from bears to whales. These brief educational clips give teachers a jumping-off point for a more in-depth lesson. The teacher puts the clip in context, and answers students' questions.

But the show is not solely for those with short attention spans. Created for use in grades K–6, *TLC Elementary School* airs every Tuesday morning from 4:00 A.M. to 5:00 A.M. (ET). This hour of programming consists of myriad 5- to 15-minute segments that can be incorporated into curriculum. Each hour has a multicultural, cross-curricular approach to the subject. One example of *TLC Elementary School* is a theme-based hour on oceans, composed of short clips about all of the planet's oceans.

The Learning Channel and the Discovery Channel fall under the umbrella of Discovery Networks in the *Cable in the Classroom* magazine. Discovery Networks puts out an educator guide for the Discovery

Channel and The Learning Channel. Call (800) 321-1832 to receive a free subscription.

Also, you don't want to miss *School Stories,* a documentary series designed to spotlight successful teaching strategies in education.

For further information, write to The Learning Channel, 7700 Wisconsin Avenue, Bethesda, Maryland 20814.

A&E Television Network and The History Channel

A&E is an arts and entertainment television network featuring an original Biography® series, mysteries, and specials. Biographies have aired on people such as Princess Grace, Tchaikovsky, Thomas Jefferson, and George Bernard Shaw. Specials topics run the gamut from the genetic revolution to the Dallas Symphony Orchestra.

The History Channel is a 24-hour television network featuring historical documentaries, movies, and miniseries. History can be found under the general curriculum category in *Cable in the Classroom* magazine. *Nippon: Japan Since 1945* is one example of a five-part series airing on The History Channel. Another example is *Civil War Journal,* an original documentary series using archival materials, photographs, and diaries to explore a turbulent period in U.S. history.

A&E Classroom offers a biannual schedule, program descriptions, and study guides. The History Channel Classroom likewise offers program descriptions and study guides. Request *The Idea Book,* a manual filled with teachers' new ideas along with study guides for using A&E and The History Channel's Cable in the Classroom programming. Write to Community Development, A&E Television Network, P.O. Box 1610, Grand Central Station, New York, NY 10163-1610.

Court TV

Court TV is listed in *Cable in the Classroom* magazine as CTN—Courtroom Television Network. This is a 24-hour basic cable network dedicated to live and taped coverage of real courtroom trials and other legal proceedings from around the country, anchored by a team of experienced attorneys and legal journalists. Court TV covers current trials as well as past trials such as the Nuremberg War Crimes Trial, which provides an historical perspective with modern relevance.

Susan Abbey, vice president of community affairs, says you don't have to teach law to use Court TV in your classroom. Also, you don't have to be a middle or high school social studies teacher. Second graders, for example can watch Court TV in English or health classes. Teachers can weave Court TV into any area of their curriculum.

CTN offers *Class Action*, a 1-hour weekly program for classroom use. It is a commercial-free program using Court TV's library of courtroom and news footage to produce programs that stimulate discussion about important social and legal issues affecting students. Issues include teenage relationship abuse, AIDS and society, and environmental concerns. Topics and study guides are available.

On Saturday and Sunday mornings, the network broadcasts Teen Court TV—3 hours of programming that explores the justice system from a young viewer's perspective and allows teenagers to participate in the programs. The three shows are *Justice Factory*, a behind-the-scenes view of our justice system; *What's the Verdict?*, an analysis of real trials; and *Your Turn*, an issues-oriented talk show with a panel of teens and experts and a studio audience of teenagers.

For more information about *Class Action* programs, call (800) 333-7649. Ask for a free study guide. You can also write to Court TV, 600 Third Avenue, New York, NY 10016.

Nickelodeon

Nickelodeon offers programs including *Nick News, Launch Box,* and *Mr. Wizard's World.* Nickelodeon is behind the Big Help, a multiyear national grassroots campaign to encourage and empower kids to perform volunteer service in their communities. The Big Help appeals to the 6- to 14-year-old audience to involve them in constructive activities.

To find out how you can get involved with Nickelodeon's Big Help, call (212) 258-7579. For further information, call the Nickelodeon Hotline at (800) 964-6425. For program scheduling, call (800)

NICKNET or write to Nick Elementary, 1515 Broadway, 21st Floor, New York, NY 10036.

Sci-Fi Channel

Sci-Fi Channel offers programming on science, technology, and space exploration. Sci-Fi Channel's *Inside Space* is a science fact series presenting the latest news about space. Your students will watch inventors and hear them discuss current projects.

Sci-Fi Channel provides materials on each episode's topic as well as suggested activities to further integrate the program into your classroom and lesson plans. Each *Inside Space* episode is approximately 30 minutes long. For *Inside Space* lesson plans, fax a request to (212) 408-9187, or write to USA Networks, Marketing, 1230 Avenue of the Americas, New York, NY 10020.

PBS

According to Sandra Welch, executive vice president at the Public Broadcasting Service (PBS) Learning Services in Alexandria, Virginia, PBS has for more than 25 years provided teachers with quality programs that have really made a difference in learning. And she assured me that teachers can count on PBS to continue providing even more and better programming in the future.

Bill Nye the Science Guy, Wishbone, The Magic School Bus (for Pre-K students), and *Nova* (for secondary students) are among the most successful PBS efforts.

The monthly guide to PBS programming with advance information for teachers is called *PBS Teacher Connex*. There is also a *CPB* (Corporation for Public Broadcasting) *Teacher's Digest* that publishes teacher-written articles about real learning in real classrooms. Call (800) 278-4176 to subscribe.

Many new electronic field trips are being offered through PBS. For further information about PBS and other local services, contact the education director or education manager at your local PBS station.

Cable in the Classroom Television Programmers and How to Reach Them

The following is a list of Cable in the Classroom members. Members have pledged to offer commercial-free educational programming with liberal copyright clearances.

A&E

> *A&E Network. Original Biography® series, mysteries, and specials. A&E Classroom, P.O. Box 1610, Grand Central Station, New York, NY 10163-1610.*

BET

> *Black Entertainment Television. Music, sports, news, and public-affairs programming. One BET Plaza, 1900 West Place NE, Washington, DC 20018; (800) 229-2388.*

BRV

> *Bravo. International films, music, and performing arts. Community Relations, 150 Crossways Park W, Woodbury, NY 11797; (516) 364-2222.*

C-SPAN/C-SPAN2

> *Live coverage of U.S. House of Representatives, U.S. Senate, and public affairs. 400 North Capitol Street NW, Suite 650, Washington, DC 20001; (202) 737-3220.*

CNBC

> *Financial and business news, and interactive talk programming. 2200 Fletcher Avenue, Fort Lee, NJ 07024; (201) 585-6469.*

CNN

> *Cable News Network. News and public affairs. Turner Educational Services, One CNN Center, Atlanta, GA 30348-5366; (404) 827-1717.*

CTN

> *Courtroom Television Network. Live and taped coverage of courtroom trials with legal analysis and discussion. Cable in the Classroom Services Department, 600 Third Avenue, New York, NY 10016; (800) 333-7649.*

DSC

Discovery Channel. Nonfiction nature, science and technology, history, and global exploration. 7700 Wisconsin Avenue, Bethesda, MD 20814-3522; (800) 321-1832.

ESPN/ESPN2

Sports programming. Cable in the Classroom Department, 935 Middle Street, Bristol, CT 06010; (203) 585-2000.

F&V

Faith & Values Channel. Dramas, documentaries, and public affairs. 74 Trinity Place, Ninth Floor, New York, NY 10006; (212) 964-1663 extension 126.

FAM

The Family Channel. Family-oriented movies, specials, and original series; health and exercise programming. 2877 Guardian Lane, P.O. Box 2050, Virginia Beach, VA 23450-2050; (804) 459-6165.

HBO

Home Box Office. Feature movies, specials, and sports programming. 1100 Avenue of the Americas, New York, NY 10036.

HIST

The History Channel. Historical documentaries, movies, and miniseries. 235 East 45th Street, Ninth Floor, New York, NY 10017; (212) 210-9780.

KNOW

Knowledge TV. Distance education, interactive field trips, language programming, and teacher training. 9697 East Mineral Avenue, Englewood, CO 80112; (800) 777-MIND.

LIFE

Lifetime. Information and entertainment programming for women. Worldwide Plaza, 309 West 49th Street, New York, NY 10019.

MSNBC

News, talk, and information network; Internet service. 2200 Fletcher Avenue, Fort Lee, NJ 07024; (201) 585-6469.

MTV

Music Television. Music, entertainment, sports, styles, news, and information for young adults. 1515 Broadway, 25th Floor, New York, NY 10036; (800) 2468-MTV.

NICK

Nickelodeon. Entertainment and educational magazine shows for children ages 2–15. Affiliate Marketing Department, 1515 Broadway, 39th Floor, New York, NY 10036; (212) 258-8000.

OVATN

Ovation. Visual arts, performing arts, and humanities for junior high-, high school-, and college-level viewing. 201 North Union Street, Suite 210, Alexandria, VA 22314; (800) 682-8466.

PBS

Public Broadcasting Service. Instructional, cultural, documentary, and news programming. Call your local PBS station, or write PBS Learning Services, 1320 Braddock Place, Alexandria, VA 22314.

SFC

Sci-Fi Channel. Science-fiction movies and series; science, technology, and space exploration programming. 1230 Avenue of the Americas, New York, NY 10020; (212) 408-9168.

SHOW

Showtime. Feature movies, sports, and specials. 1633 Broadway, New York, NY 10019.

TLC

The Learning Channel. Documentary history, science, human behavior, how-to, and children's programming. 7700 Wisconsin Avenue, Bethesda, MD 20814-3522; (800) 321-1832.

TOON

Cartoon Network. Cartoon series and feature-length animation programming. Turner Educational Services, One CNN Center, Atlanta, GA 30348-5366; (404) 827-1717.

TRAVEL

The Travel Channel. Series, specials, updates, and special-events coverage, with a geographical perspective. 2690 Cumberland Parkway, Suite 500, Atlanta, GA 30339; (770) 801-2400.

TVFN

Television Food Network. Entertaining and informative programming on cooking and nutrition. 1177 Avenue of the Americas, New York, NY 10036.

TWC

The Weather Channel. Local, regional, and national weather; meteorological specials. Education Services, 2600 Cumberland Parkway, Atlanta, GA 30339; (800) 471-5544.

USA

USA Network. Movies, specials, sports, and series. 1230 Avenue of the Americas, New York, NY 10020; (212) 408-9168.

WAM

WAM! Programming on natural sciences, social studies, literature, and teen issues. America's Youth Network, Encore, 5445 DTC Parkway, Suite 600, Englewood, CO 80111; (303) 771-7700.

WGN

WGN/UVTV. Movies, series, specials, sports, children's shows, and original programming. One Technology Plaza, 7140 South Lewis Avenue, Tulsa, OK 74136-5422; (800) 331-4806.

Note: Some programming services may not be available in all areas.

Cable TV as a
Teaching Tool

Using *Cable in the Classroom* Magazine

Your road map to cable programming is *Cable in the Classroom* magazine. This monthly publication highlights all of the commercial-free educational programming for the month. Every issue showcases at least one educator and details how he or she used cable programming in a novel way. These features might spark off some ideas about how you can use it in your own classroom.

To subscribe to *Cable in the Classroom* magazine, call (800) 216-2225 or write to Cable in the Classroom, 86 Elm Street, Peterborough, NH 03458. In the meantime, your local cable company representative can arrange for a free workshop from a Cable in the Classroom representative.

Cable in the Classroom magazine should be highlighted, dog-eared, and read over and over again. This is not a magazine to skim through, only to shelve or discard it. The magazine is divided by subject and curriculum areas. I recommend reading about all of the programming. You may find something in the English curriculum area and use it in history instead. Likewise, just because something is labeled American history doesn't mean it can't be used in art class.

Also, don't worry about grade levels. There are things you can do to tailor programs to your class. For example, many elementary school teachers turn the sound off and have children create their own audio for a program that uses vocabulary words at a higher grade level. The trick is to read through the magazine with an open mind.

How to Read *Cable in the Classroom* Magazine

1. Take out the taping calendar highlights centerfold. Laminate it and post it in your classroom.
2. Go to your curriculum area and match programs to your units.
3. Review all other curriculum areas to look for matches. Take your time.
4. Look at the grant information. Consider teaming up with other teachers. For a recent Continental Cablevision Award, for instance, a team of teachers from Michigan—two high school teachers and one elementary teacher—won.
5. Read educator stories for hints. They can be inspiring.

Matching Cable Television to Classroom Curriculum

Which comes first, Cable in the Classroom programming or your curriculum? It's totally up to you. Cable in the Classroom programs are crafted to match curriculum frameworks in the United States. But you use them however you want.

As I read *Cable in the Classroom* magazine, I look for programming to supplement my curriculum. I read with a particular unit in mind and brainstorm every possible way I can use a program with my students. For example, if you are teaching a butterfly unit, you would look under science to see if there was something geared for that branch of science. If you are doing a multimedia presentation, you may need a moving picture of a butterfly, so you could videotape a clip of a butterfly in a rain forest. You could even tape a clip from the opera *Madame Butterfly*.

There is always something in the magazine to match your curriculum. It takes a little practice as well as time. The summer issue, July/August, comes out at the beginning of July. This is a great time to start preparing for fall classes.

Be creative. After about my 10th time reviewing the programming, curriculum connections start jumping out at me that I hadn't seen before. Mike Leone, director of government and public affairs of Continental Cablevision of New England, told me that the best example he had ever heard of concerned a kindergarten teacher who used a series on A&E called *Dinosaurs*, hosted by Walter Cronkite.

Traditionally, teachers use this program to supplement a lesson on dinosaurs. However, this teacher had a completely different idea. She used this program to reinforce a lesson on proper dental hygiene. When the dinosaur opened his mouth, the teacher would freeze that frame and use a giant toothbrush to demonstrate the up-and-down brushing strokes that children should use when brushing their teeth.

Integration Information

As a computer teacher, I teach language arts skills, but with a flick of the mouse, I'm reinforcing math skills. I use geography software along with multimedia applications. I am *always* teaching. When I see a student drop trash on the floor, I teach environmental concern. I wear dozens of hats all day long, as do all teachers. We seek teaching opportunities all the time.

This mind-set in particular pertains to lesson planning. When planning for the unit Computers in the Community, I consider appropriate vocabulary, the history of computers, a field experience, visits from people who use computers in their jobs, cable television programming on computers, taking apart a computer, writing about computers, finding an Internet project, and drawing what computers will look like in the future. Well-rounded lessons involve every possible angle you can incorporate. It's like brainstorming to the nth degree. When I did a penguin unit, I suddenly had an overwhelming urge to visit the New England Aquarium to observe and photograph penguins. When I did a unit called Chocolate Technology, I turned into a chef and baked chocolate goodies.

Talk to other teachers. Talk to your family, friends, and anyone who will listen. Develop an integration network. It is easier to find ways to integrate if you brainstorm with others than if you do it all alone.

My mother, a retired teacher, is my so-called "integration scout." She carries a list of my units with her in her pocketbook and when she sees something or meets someone she feels will enhance my curriculum, her integration radar sounds. She helps me cover yet another interdisciplinary base.

When she sewed a farm apron adorned with a red barn, horse, and cow, I realized I was onto something. I now dress for my units. I use puppets, hats, masks, and wigs to add drama and fantasy to my lessons. These teaching tools add another dimension to what I am teaching. One of my favorite things to do is take out my yellow pom-poms, and shake them in front of the class and in the back of the class when I teach. The kids listen and learn.

I think of cable television as a window to the world and another tool to stimulate students and complement what I'm already doing. My situation is not perfect. I don't have a VCR that can tape programs in the computer lab so I do my taping at home. I don't have The Learning Channel in my community so I have to have someone in a neighboring town tape those programs for me. (It's my cousin Beth, and, of course, she ends up watching the shows.)

You have to have an idea, but not necessarily a finalized plan, as to where cable television fits in. Jot down subject areas such as science, math, language arts, and history, and make the connections. Software applications that allow you to create flow charts on the computer are helpful.

Talk to the art teacher. Talk to the music teacher. You may think a computer–music connection in an elementary school is a stretch, but I have my first graders sing songs about pressing the return key to go to the next line and we use musical instruments in the computer lab. I hear my students singing what they have to do next, and I know they're learning and *retaining* knowledge.

As a computer teacher, I fully understand the importance and necessity of staff development. The Discovery Network and some of the other networks offer free workshops to instruct teachers on how to use cable television in all areas of education. *Cable in the Classroom* magazine and cable television network support materials offer suggestions for taking cable television across your curriculum.

During a relaxed roundtable discussion on a hot July afternoon, I learned that the half dozen members of our group are always making connections and finding ways to apply them to their curriculum. They think about it in the morning and even dream about it at night. Immediately, I felt comforted that it wasn't just me.

Teachers need to talk about teaching tools such as cable television. They need to talk about it on a wider scale for schoolwide projects. Talking about it is a first step on the road to using it.

As a teacher who uses as many tools as I can, my days—and now years—of teaching are incredibly fulfilling. I am constantly learning, and I welcome new teaching tools into my life. I'm not bored, and my students aren't bored. We have found so much more to explore. The cable television window in my classroom is wide open. I encourage you to open yours and take one curriculum area, one subject at a time.

Nancy O'Donnell, Social Studies Teacher, Saint Joan of Arc Elementary School, Aberdeen, Maryland; C-SPAN in the Classroom Equipment Grant Winner. Nancy is always on the lookout for cable programming. She thinks that most teachers know well ahead of time what they are going to be covering that year. She recommends that they pick three or four separate things that they are going to stress and take them across the curriculum, but warns that they will have to be well prepared for that. "You have to think well in advance when you are going to be teaching a certain thing," says Nancy. "You have to figure out how you can bring those different things into play in order to pique the kids' interest."

Tips to Integrate Cable Programming Across Your Curriculum

1. *Watch the program once for content.*
2. *Watch the program with colleagues.* Ask each person to look for a different content area.
3. *Don't reinvent the wheel.* Go on-line and see what other teachers are doing with this program. Plan to adapt their ideas to accommodate your needs.
4. *Start with a lesson or project with a two-way combination—for example, history and music.* Then, as you get more comfortable, branch out.
5. *Schedule a workshop to help put cable in your school.* Call your local cable company and request a Cable in the Classroom workshop.

Developing a Lesson Using Cable Television

Taffy Patton, manager of education outreach at *Cable in the Classroom* magazine, says that the initiative's purpose is not to add paperwork or to complicate one's job. It is to facilitate one's job as an educator—to make it easier to grab a student's attention and hold it long enough to teach your state curriculum requirements. It is a classroom tool just like a computer or pencil.

I am the kind of teacher who is always looking for ways to capture my kids' attention and have them learn more. I play music, bring in guest speakers, do outdoor activities, and disguise my voice. I have always felt I was competing with television, but now I feel as though we are working together as a team to help students learn. Students are used to fast-paced, in-color, and highly produced television. Cable in the Classroom is a natural extension of what they're used to, and they quickly relate to the content.

Taffy says that in order to prevent the Cable in the Classroom initiative from becoming time-consuming or cumbersome, one should get a few parents or students to do some of the taping for you. Then you will need only to preview the tapes to determine which ones are relevant to your unit. Having a tech squad, student council, or parents participate in this manner is a fine way to save teacher time.

Developing a lesson that integrates cable TV is the same as developing any other classroom lesson. The goal, as always, is to use whatever resources are available to get a message across to one's students. And one doesn't have to use a whole program—there is no obligation to use more of a program than you actually need to teach the concept.

According to Taffy, there is no such thing as "wrong use" of Cable in the Classroom programming. She suggests that one simply use it the way it makes sense in terms of one's lesson plans. Each teacher knows the attention span of his or her students, and therefore will instinctively know which parts of a program to fast-forward through.

Steps to Developing a Lesson Using Cable Television Programming

1. Peruse *Cable in the Classroom* magazine.
2. Select a program or possibly a series of programs to use in your unit.

3. Go on-line, call, or write to request support materials. There are hundreds, perhaps thousands, of lessons already designed for you to use with Cable in the Classroom programming.
4. Record the program, or have someone do it for you.
5. Preview the program.
6. Tailor the lessons that networks provide to meet the needs of your students.

Snow Feet

Here is one of the lesson plans I submitted for my winning Continental Cablevision entry.

Title: Snow Feet.

Time: One 45-minute class period.

Grade: 2.

Objective: The goal of this lesson is to help children learn about measurement by showing how 1 foot equals 12 inches.

Materials: The Weather Channel, computers, writing software with graphic capabilities, and a ruler for each student.

Background: During the East coast's Blizzard of 1996, snow was the topic of conversation, so I capitalized on this and incorporated it into curriculum.

Procedure: Students enter the computer lab and The Weather Channel is turned on. We watch the weather and estimate how much snow is on the ground by holding up one ruler. Is there more or less than one ruler? The children respond, "More." I hold up two rulers, lined up from end to end, and then three. We estimate 3 feet of snow is on the ground.

While watching The Weather Channel, we see a meteorologist talking about snow. Vocabulary words such as *map, forecast,* and *temperature* are introduced. We line up 12 children and tell them each child represents 1 inch. The children return to their computers and write sentences. The teacher first writes the following sentence on the board as a model: "We have three feet of snow on the ground." Children write their own sentences and are encouraged to use their weather vocabulary.

Conclusion: The combination of television and computers encourages learning.

Classroom Viewing Tips: Suggestions for Teachers

1. *Plan your lesson.* What is your objective? How does this video support your objective? What new concepts and vocabulary will your students need to learn? What activities can you create to accompany the program that will enhance comprehension and reinforce or extend the new concepts? How will you evaluate what students have learned?

2. *Preview the program.* Is the program suitable for your needs? What parts of the program are relevant to your curriculum? At what point in your plans will the video be useful? A video should be a teaching tool, not a reward or a baby-sitter.

3. *Set up your videotape.* Show only the best parts. You needn't show an hour-long documentary if only one or two 5-minute segments really fit your needs. Use your VCR's tape counter to allow you to easily fast-forward or rewind to the appropriate section.

4. *Prepare your students.* Discuss what you are about to watch with them. Go over any advanced concepts or vocabulary. Some teachers find outlines and worksheets useful to focus students' attention during a video. Assign students something to look for or evaluate; a purpose or goal will make them active viewers and they will be more likely to recall what they have seen.

5. *Position yourself.* You should be near the VCR or have a remote to control the machine. You should also be in a position to monitor the class. Do *not* do other work while the video is running; that implies you do not consider the program worthwhile. And leave the lights on. Kids can see the TV just fine and are less likely to fall asleep or get restless.

6. *Pause and explain.* Stopping the tape lets you explain and emphasize key points, and check student comprehension. It also keeps them alert. You can stop to prepare students for something important that is coming up or to ask them to predict what will happen. Pausing gives students time to absorb new information, process it, and relate it to prior knowledge. You may wish to show key segments twice. Find out how students' comprehension and impressions have changed after a second exposure.

7. *Pose a question.* As soon as the tape ends, ask a prepared question that will reinforce what the students have just seen. Ask if they

can apply a newly learned concept to another situation. Take time to answer students' questions and review the important information you wanted them to gather from the program.

A Word on Assessment

You don't grade students on watching television. You assess your students on their ability to retain and apply the major ideas of the subject you are teaching. Television is a tool to help you teach, so your methods of assessment need not be any different than those you've used in the past.

Cable Television and Internet Connections

The use of the Internet by teachers is slowly growing. Goals 2000 is the president's project to hook up every classroom to the Internet by the year 2000. Cable companies all across the United States are quickly giving classrooms and public libraries Internet connections.

The Internet can enhance the value of the Cable in the Classroom initiative. Just a few years ago, the Internet was starting to develop as a tool through which teachers could get information, send messages, and contact one another. Today, cable programs are being produced with on-line support materials.

The Internet is not just a school-based "place." Soon, everyone will be able to access the Internet from a modem on TV, so any existing roadblocks or barriers are quickly disappearing. Within a year or two, using the Internet likely will be as normal or routine as owning an answering machine or sending a fax is today.

When I met with Pat Koravos, the Education On-line manager for the Discovery Channel, she walked me through the Discovery Channel School Web site, which is continually adding new features in its aim to meet the needs of teachers.

As we arrived at the home page, we were greeted by Sam the Owl, the Discovery School's mascot, and a group of teachers with more than 200 years of teaching experience combined. (Smack dab in the center of the teacher group photo was Pat!)

I clicked on Sam the Owl and was led to a listing of Discovery Channel programs. The program in which I was most interested was *Understanding Computers*, which had aired last spring. Even though the show is geared toward secondary students, I was looking for ways to use it with fourth graders.

Next, I was greeted by a teacher who gave me a list of ideas of what to do with *Understanding Computers* with secondary-level students. If I taught older students, I might have taken notes and clicked on all of the buttons that would link me to more project ideas, lessons, and background information, and then logged off.

But because I was primarily interested in using this with younger children, I linked to the Grade K–5 areas. This was further broken down to Grades K–2 and 3–5. The user-friendly eyes of the on-screen teacher gave me the impression of dealing with a real person. The teacher suggested two activities: (a) Have students write a story about life with a new robot, and (b) plan a virtual tour to the nation's capitol.

Just think of all the time I would have spent reinventing the wheel, putting hours into designing lessons from scratch. This was sharing at its most efficient!

Every time Discovery Channel produces a program, all 50 state curriculum guidelines are consulted. You can open a textbook, match it up with any one of the Discovery programs, and find the stated objectives and program highlights on-line. There are also teacher support materials that can be printed out from the Internet, photocopied, and distributed.

Its Web site allows you to send any of the on-line teachers e-mail with questions about the cable program. You can ask questions about the use of the program in a classroom or any educational issue that crops up. You can expect to receive a timely response within 1 to 3 days.

On-Line Addresses

Don't miss *Cable in the Classroom*'s Web site! This is a resource for teachers that offers, among other things, a searchable database of the magazine's program listings. Following are World Wide Web addresses for cable networks and programs.

A&E

http://www.aetv.com

Look for program schedules and descriptions, copyright information, free support materials, and classroom resources.

BET

http://www.betnetworks.com

Bravo

http://www.bravotv.com

Look for program schedules and descriptions and free support materials.

Cable in the Classroom

http://www.ciconline.com

Cartoon Network

http://www.filmzone.com/SpaceGhost/cartoonnet.html

From America Online, enter keyword: cartoon

Look for program schedules and descriptions, free support materials, and the ability to post messages.

CNBC

http://www.cnbc.com

CNN

http://www.cnn.com

From America Online, enter keyword: cnn

Look for CNN Newsroom/CNN Worldview *program schedules and descriptions, daily classroom guides, classroom materials (e.g., photos, maps, documents, and audio and video clips), and on-line interactivity (users can post messages and suggestions and participate in chat rooms and moderated on-line discussions).*

Court TV

http://www.courttv.com

From America Online, enter keyword: courttv

From Prodigy, jump: courttv

Look for schedules and descriptions, free lesson plans, and support materials for Class Action. Classroom materials found on-line include maps, photos, charts, documents, and software. Educators and students can post messages and suggestions and participate in discussions and moderated on-line debates.

C-SPAN

http://www.c-span.org

From America Online, enter keyword: c-span

From Microsoft Network, go to: C-Span

Look for program listings with descriptions and copyright information, free support materials (e.g., maps, photos, charts, original documents, audio clips), and on-line interactivity (e.g., a message board, chat rooms, moderated on-line discussions, and a suggestion box).

Discovery Channel

http://school.discovery.com

From America Online, enter keyword: dsc-ed

Look for program schedules and descriptions (including those for Assignment Discovery). There are free lesson plans, support materials, audio and visual aids, and documents. There is a message board and a teacher chat room.

ESPN/ESPN2

http://espnet.sportszone.com

From Microsoft Network, go to: espnet sportszone

From Prodigy, jump: espnet

Look for program schedules, audio and visual resources, chat rooms, and a suggestion box.

The Family Channel

http://www.famfun.com

From CompuServe, go to: ydrive

Look for program schedules and descriptions.

HBO

http://www.homebox.com

The History Channel

http://www.historychannel.com

Look for program schedules and descriptions, including the History Channel Classroom, free support materials, video and audio classroom resources, and a suggestion box.

Knowledge TV

http://www.jec.edu

Look for undergraduate and graduate distance education opportunities.

The Learning Channel

http://school.discovery.com

From America Online, enter keyword: tlc-ed

Look for program schedules and descriptions, copyright information, free lesson plans and support materials, audio and visual aids, and documents.

Lifetime

http://www.lifetimetv.com

Look for program schedules and descriptions.

MTV

http://www.mtv.com

From America Online, enter keyword: MTV

Look for program listings and descriptions, audio and video clips, on-line discussions, and the ability to post messages.

Nickelodeon

From America Online, enter keyword: Nickelodeon

Ovation

http://www.ovationtv.com

Look for support materials, including lesson plans, suggested activities, and advance program schedules.

PBS

http://www.pbs.org

Look for program schedules and descriptions, free lesson plans, support materials, activity sheets, and other classroom aids (e.g., photos, charts, original documents, and video and audio clips). Interactive elements include a message board, moderated discussions, and a suggestion box.

Sci-Fi Channel

http://www.scifi.com

Look for program schedules and descriptions, lesson plans (including those for Inside Space), and free support materials. You can post messages and suggestions.

Showtime

http://www.showtimeonline.com

Look for program listings and descriptions.

USA

http://www.usanetwork.com

Look for programming schedules and descriptions, along with support materials.

The Weather Channel

http://www.weather.com/weather

From CompuServe, go: TWCForum

Look for program schedules and descriptions, lesson plans, and support materials (available for free and for purchase). Interactivity is provided through a suggestion box, message board, chat rooms, and moderated on-line discussions.

WGN/UVTV

http://www.uvtv.com

Look for program schedules, support materials, a message board, and live chat rooms.

Although this list of Web sites is as up-to-date as possible, I suggest that you contact any unlisted networks in your area to request their Internet addresses as they become available.

Teacher Training Opportunities

Many of the cable television networks will send someone to your school to conduct a workshop. All you have to do is call and ask what is offered. Refer to the list of networks in Chapter 4. Teachers who have been using Cable in the Classroom effectively will visit your school and make it come alive for you.

For example, if you want to learn more about the Discovery Channel or The Learning Channel, call (800) 321-1832. Since 1992, when they began training teachers, about 30,000 educators have been trained. They now have what is called a VCR team, a group of educators who visit schools across the country explaining how to use Discovery Network programming in classrooms.

Teacher Josie Levine, a Discovery On-line educator for the Discovery Networks, stresses that these workshops are free. VCR team members will visit your school gratis—you decide the length of the presentation. Qualified team members come equipped with years of teaching experience and are more than willing to share what has worked for them and what has not.

If you don't have access to The Learning Channel, Josie will discuss the Discovery Channel. If you would like a free workshop in your school, it's simple. Contact your local cable company to arrange a Cable in the Classroom workshop. That's all there is to it.

To find out which cable company can sponsor a workshop in your area, call (703) 845-1400.

Teacher Training Opportunities

There are two great resources in which you should seriously consider participating.

The first is called the Technology + Learning Conference, and you can find out more about it through the National School Boards Association, 1680 Duke Street, Alexandria, VA 22314-3493, or call (800) 950-6722.

The second is the J. C. Sparkman Center for Educational Technology, which is operated by Tele-Communications. It offers hands-on training with a variety of cable-delivered resources and other technologies. The Center offers free on-site training for educators located in or visiting the Denver area, and training sessions are also available nationwide via satellite. For information, write to the J. C. Sparkman Center for Educational Technology, 4100 East Dry Creek Road, Room 125, Littleton, CO 80122, or call (303) 267-6700.

Twelve Tips for Effective Television Use

1. Never turn off the lights in the classroom.
2. Preview tapes.
3. Develop previewing activities.
4. Pause.
5. Rewind.
6. Stop and start.
7. Question.
8. Use focusing activities.
9. Engage students in postshow activities.
10. Make use of segmented viewing.
11. Plan for purposeful viewing.
12. Enjoy!

Copyright Basics

There are many different interpretations of copyright law regarding educational use of television. The best-known doctrine is that of *fair use*, which was originally based on broadcast TV. Fair use allows taping for educational purposes, as long as the tapes are shown only once within 10 days of taping and are erased after 45 days. However, Cable in the Classroom members—the cable television networks listed in Chapter 4—have purchased or contractually arranged for copyright clearances that extend beyond fair use on all Cable in the Classroom programs and many other shows. All blue titles in *Cable in the Classroom* magazine's listings have copyright clearances beyond fair use; most are 1 year or longer.

Each cable network has made its own legal interpretation of the copyright restrictions on its programs, and that interpretation is indicated by the copyright code below the program's title in *Cable in the Classroom* listings. All programming on C-SPAN is copyright cleared for educational use. BET and CNBC have cleared copyrights on all programs produced in-house. Court TV has cleared all programming for 1 year. Prime-time programs on A&E, Bravo, and Lifetime are subject to fair use, and PBS copyrights tend to be fair use or longer.

Copyright-restricted programs, identified by the code RES, may be taped for home use. These can be shown in public when they air, but cannot be taped for future public viewing (including viewing in schools). There are two main reasons that copyright-restricted programs are listed: (a) Teachers may want to assign them as homework or extra credit or watch them for their own continuing education; and (b) many restricted programs are available for purchase on videotape (as indicated by the VIDEO AVAIL. code).

The information printed in *Cable in the Classroom* magazine regarding copyrights is not legal advice. It consists of interpretations by nonattorneys of a complex set of imprecise guidelines.

The following organizations can help you understand copyright laws.

Association for Educational Communications & Technology (AECT)
1025 Vermont Avenue NW, Suite 820
Washington, DC 20005
(202) 347-7834
Numerous publications on copyright are available to purchase.

Association for Information Media and Equipment (AIME)
P.O. Box 1173
56 John Street
Clarksdale, MS 38614
Call (601) 624-9355 or fax (601) 624-9366.

In *Cable in the Classroom* magazine, look for the copyright codes under the title of the program listing to determine how long tapes may be saved. Or scan the listings for blue titles—these have extended educational copyright clearances. In addition, all programs on the pullout calendar may be taped.

Copyright Codes

FREE: Unrestricted use of tape for educational purposes.

3 YRS: Show within 3 years.

YEAR: Show within 1 year.

SEM: Show during the semester in which the program was taped.

FAIR: Fair Use: Show within 10 days; tape may be saved for reference for 45 days.

WEEK: Show within 7 days.

RES: Restricted: May be taped for home use only. Tapes may not be replayed publicly in school.

NA: Information not available at press time.

Contests and Grants

Cable in the Classroom magazine has an entire page devoted to contest and grant announcements and winners. Contests are wonderful. Winning contests opens doors. It puts you in touch with other innovative educators, and you may be invited to attend events or join organizations you didn't know existed. In my case, it provided me with a life experience I will always remember.

The contest I won is Continental Cablevision's National Cable Educator Award, which honors teachers around the country for their innovative use of cable television programming and technology in the classroom. They have sponsored this contest for the past 7 years.

The Continental Cable Educator Award application asks for a project's description, its objectives, and how it benefits children. It is a short, simple form to complete—nothing like most grant applications I've seen!

Mike Leone, director of government and public affairs of Continental Cablevision of New England, is one of the committee members who selected my application from the pool of applicants. He told me I was chosen for my integrated approach to using cable programming and computer technology.

Tips for Winning Cable Contests and Grants

1. *Read the rules.* Many teachers send in the same grant application for 50 different grants. They don't read the rules and take the time to determine what is required.
2. *Type your entry even if typing isn't a requirement.* These things make a difference in terms of presentation when submitted.
3. *Include support materials,* such as copies of lesson plans, videotapes, and newspaper clippings (if your project has had any press coverage). The judges really like to see these items.

According to Larry Pratt, an education outreach specialist at C-SPAN, these contests and grants are not necessarily as competitive as you might think. His single piece of advice is to write up a project that is working for you in the classroom and submit it.

Tips From Continental Cablevision National Cable Educator Award Winners

The best part of winning a trip to Washington, D.C., was meeting the other Continental Cablevision Educator award winners. It isn't enough just to read about their finished projects. I spoke to winning educators individually, and each had his or her own unique story to tell. They were more than willing to share strategies and give advice to other teachers.

You may think every cable award winner is a superhuman who has the best cable access in the world and doesn't face any obstacles. But the truth is they are not superhuman and they face obstacles along the way—just like you and me.

When I first began writing this chapter, I planned to include only three or four educators and their outstanding projects. But I couldn't stop after those first few interviews. As I listened and took notes, I was learning. This chapter highlights winners from across the country.

Marla Gartner, Teacher, Ealy Elementary School, West Bloomfield, Michigan. With technical support from Continental, a live interactive video teleconference on the physics of sound and music was broadcast to all schools within Michigan's intermediate school district.

Viewers were encouraged to phone in questions and discover the answers through hands-on experiments and demonstrations.

Marla and her two colleagues, Paul Drummond and Joseph Hoffman, decided to produce their own program rather than use a cable-produced program because they found out they had limited cable access in their schools. They focused on physics and combined it with music, art, science, math, and language arts.

Marla reached out into the community so children could see how sound and music apply to real-life situations. Some children worked with their music teachers to create instruments. They learned how sound is produced. Then they composed their own songs, which they played on their handmade instruments.

When learning about acoustics, Marla and her students visited homes with and without carpeting to demonstrate how sound changes. She took one group of students to the Detroit Symphony, and the students actually played with the symphony inside Music Hall.

One segment of the teleconference featured the school choir performing in three different locations: a synagogue, the outdoors, and a bus. The choir sang the same song in these three locations. During the teleconference, people voted for the place in which the song sounded better. As it turned out, it sounded better in the school bus, although it was expected to have sounded best in the synagogue. They deduced that sound bouncing off the empty temple walls was detrimental to the results.

Tip: *One way to overcome limited cable access is to create your own program. You can even design your own teacher-activity books.*

Joseph Hoffman, Teacher, West Bloomfield High School, West Bloomfield, Michigan. As a physics teacher, Joe uses PBS's *Nova* programming to bring science to a point where everyone can understand it. He also uses The Weather Channel to make complex phenomena understandable. Joe discussed some of the tools teachers can use: books, videotapes, computers, labs, and televisions. He uses cable programming to show students recent science developments and to demonstrate that all things in science don't have to be historic. TV provides him with real data and real-time, real-world science.

Joe always writes for support materials. He uses teacher's guides for *Nova* programs. He says they offer a good fundamental base for what the program is going to be about and provide him with discussion points and questions to consider.

> Tip: *We tend to invest a lot of time in day-to-day planning for class, correcting papers, and building relationships with kids. Cable television is another avenue in which it would be worthwhile to invest. Instead of giving a homework assignment that will take hours to correct, use that time to seek out creative cable programming.*

Paul Drummond, Teacher, Ealy Elementary School, West Bloomfield, Michigan. Paul is a fifth-grade teacher and science coordinator. When he created a parent's group in 1994 to expand his Young Astronaut Student Club, he never imagined this would result in taking part in shuttle radio communication with the astronauts aboard the Endeavor.

A parent in this group, which he called the Pathfinders, led him to a radio enthusiast, who in turn led him to a NASA grant. Paul wasn't discouraged when he heard that many people apply. He knew if he didn't apply, he definitely *wouldn't* get it. As it turned out, his school was one of nine schools in the world selected.

The Pathfinders produced a televised program about making contact with the shuttle. By televising it via a cable network, they were able to broadcast it throughout the Detroit metropolitan area and share it with millions. The program was interactive, meaning that viewers called in with questions.

This multidistrict teleconference, Shuttle in Motion, was nominated for a Smithsonian Computer Award, and Paul's school was inducted into the Smithsonian in the spring of 1995.

> Tip: *Make connections with parents and people who are working in the real world because many want to be involved.*

Richard Benz, Teacher and Media Specialist, Wickliffe High School, Wickliffe, Ohio. Students in Richard's biology class used CNN and the Internet to research deadly Ebola-type viruses and investigate how a major event like the Ebola outbreak is tied to world politics as well as the global economy.

Richard wears the hats of biology teacher, science chairman, and director of technology. Some of his other awards include a 1994 Disney Teacher of the Year Award in Science; a 1993 Ohio Milken Educator Award for $25,000, which he used to travel to the Galapagos Islands and buy video equipment; and a 1990 Presidential Award for Science Teaching. Richard does workshops and presentations across the country at national science and technology conferences.

He has been involved in teaching with cable television for 9 years. For his Continental Cablevision entry, he wanted to come up with something timely and significant. At the time, news reports about the Ebola outbreak in Zaire were coming in just about every day. As a codirector of a project called Science Across America, he was invited to go to Africa to work with African educators to start Science Across Africa. Richard said the Ebola virus and trip to Africa popped up together in his mind and he decided to have his students investigate Ebola-type diseases.

> Tip: *Build your treasure chest of teaching resources. Cable television is one of the best.*

Kevin Sacerdote, Paxon College Preparatory School, Jacksonville, Florida. Using A&E's Biography® series, laser discs, and books, Kevin's students researched the life of Michelangelo, his works, and the political and religious power structure from which the European Renaissance period emanated.

In addition to the Continental Award, Kevin also won a C-SPAN Equipment for Education grant and a 1-month fellowship at C-SPAN in Washington, D.C., wherein he represented high school teachers from across the nation and worked with the C-SPAN education staff.

His Continental Award–winning project was for his work with students in his advanced-placement European history class. He used an A&E Biography® on Michelangelo called *Artist and Man*. He found this under the arts section of *Cable in the Classroom* magazine rather than the social studies section.

Kevin calls his teaching style interdisciplinary and well-rounded. For example, his discussions about the history of humankind include literature, geography, and mathematics. He feels that with a little bit of digging, one can find more than enough to kick the doors open in all the different fields.

> Tip: *Network! Don't be afraid to ask other teachers—your peers—about their perspectives on topics you'd like to explore with your students.*

Frank Watson, Teacher, Plantation High School, Plantation, Florida. Frank's 9th- and 10th-grade social studies students used *CNN Newsroom* to learn about different cultures in the world, their contributions to U.S. society, and their role in world events. While incorporating these ideas into class debates, speeches, and group discussion, students developed analytical and problem-solving skills, as well as an appreciation of ethnic differences.

Frank's school is equipped with TVs and VCRs in every classroom. His winning project for Continental Cablevision extended the research he did when working on his doctorate in education at Nova Southeastern University in Florida. This research focused on critical thinking and how to improve the achievement and interest of all students. He advocates student exposure to different instructional modalities such as CNN.

He wanted to win this contest because it would give his students a big boost to know they were involved in a cutting-edge project. According to Frank, we are moving toward an age in which students must be exposed to technology at any cost. He encourages teachers to take advantage of technology that is available to them because they are not only enhancing their individual curriculum but also preparing students for the 21st century.

> Tip: *Entering and winning contests can benefit your students.*

Kathy Bruni, Teacher, Butler Junior High School, Oak Brook, Illinois. A&E's Biography® and 20th Century programs served as sources of information for Kathy's language arts and public speaking students who used videos and computers to create multimedia presentations.

Kathy's main area of language arts is public speaking, and every year she teaches seventh-grade students how to write a manuscript speech.

Kathy's students selected major events and public figures of the 20th century and did extensive research on their chosen interests. As they read and became immersed in the writing process, their essays grew into manuscripts, which they were taught to mark as an actor would a script.

Students were then videotaped as they delivered their speeches, which ranged from 4 to 10 minutes.

Students also implanted video clips from cable television programming and created videotaped speeches. Speech topics included the Titanic, Eleanor Roosevelt, and John F. Kennedy.

All of their speeches are stored in individual binders with the project title on its spine. At this point, Kathy has more than 100 binders on display in her classroom. Visiting educators and parents who attend open house enjoy perusing the binders.

Kathy uses *Cable in the Classroom* magazine as part of her monthly planning. As soon as she receives it, she laminates the calendar and posts it beside the VCR in her classroom where her students can refer to it. Her students are responsible for videotaping clips related to a topic they are interested in researching.

She finds cable television to be a wonderful medium to accommodate different learning styles. She feels auditory learners enjoy a new comfort level just when they see the television is on. She says it makes these students want to participate more.

> Tip: *Television complements language arts curriculum. Cable adds a new dimension to the writing process.*

Cheryl Jensen, Teacher, John F. Kennedy High School, La Palma, California. Cheryl Jensen is a high school teacher *without* cable access to Court TV in her school who still managed to win a Continental Cablevision award along with a national Court TV equipment grant in the same year. How did she do it?

Determined to complement her multicultural issues course with cable programming, she overcame this access obstacle by purchasing the videotape *Getting Physical: How Relationship Abuse Is Affecting Teenagers* through Court TV. Cheryl's students then explored their own experiences with violence. They participated in spirited, intense class discussion and engaged in imaginary letter-writing exercises to victims and perpetrators of abuse.

Cheryl, an art teacher for 27 years, is the department chair. Her involvement in teaching culturally themed programs in the art department led to the birth of her multicultural issues course, a discussion-based class dealing with contemporary topics and designed to honor the many cultures in her school.

Cheryl uses support materials as a springboard for her units. She feels they can be very helpful, especially for teachers just beginning to integrate cable into their curriculum. She cautions against using a video with a worksheet as students will tend to watch for answers to the worksheet rather than view critically. She recommends that children watch the videotape and then be asked to reflect.

Cheryl distributed a written evaluation form to the students 2 weeks after showing the videotape, with questions about personal impact, life changes, and how they plan to apply what they've learned. Many of the students mentioned the video in their own evaluation, and generally found it quite powerful.

In her classroom with its multiage groupings of students with different levels of ability and a host of learning styles, she feels cable television is an excellent tool. To encourage other teachers in her school to use cable, she invites them to cable conferences. As a result of this effort, more and more teachers in her school are using cable. Cheryl says staff development is the key to keeping teachers current with new ways of teaching, and this includes the adoption of cable television as a tool.

According to Cheryl, one misconception some teachers have about cable television is that they feel it is necessary to show students an entire program. But Cheryl insists that cable programming must be interactive for it to be genuinely effective. She says a teacher has to use video as a catalyst for discussion, break it down into a number of segments, pause for discussion purposes, and act as a facilitator in the classroom.

Tip: *There are creative ways of getting around limited or nonexistent cable access in your school.*

Manuel Moreno, Teacher, Lincoln High School, Stockton, California. Students in Manuel's anatomy and physiology classes at Lincoln High School incorporate medical programming from The Learning Channel into a live weekly program they produce for seventh- and eighth-grade students. The program is distributed through Continental's two-way broadband network, which allows visual and audio interaction among students at separate campuses.

The interactive television show is called *Body Dynamics,* and in it Manuel's high school students conduct lessons for K–8 students in real time. One group of students did in-depth research on acne. According to Manuel, to have a high school student talk to a seventh or eighth grader about acne is powerful—it confirms that almost all the high school students have it and know how it feels.

The students discuss what they learned in their research. The acne project, for instance, included visuals (such as models to show the skin layers and glands). Manuel said this experience allowed the high school students to be great role models and to show that learning is fun. It empowered them because they were ready to answer any questions posed by viewers, and this increased their self-esteem. He said this project was (a) building a bridge from eighth to ninth grade, and (b) reinforcing the attitude before coming to high school that "learning is cool."

This year, Manuel is busy working toward his goal of setting up an interactive cable television studio in the library. He hopes teachers will be able to do basically the same thing he did, but in their respective disciplines.

Tip: *All the different technologies are nice additives to the pot. They enhance learning.*

Jay Roy, Rollinsford Grade School, Rollinsford, New Hampshire. Jay's fifth- and sixth-grade students used *CNN Newsroom* and video literacy tools (such as Continental's *Classroom Guide to Master Control— Television Literacy for Kids* programming on production techniques) to understand all facets of video production before creating a video yearbook.

Jay entered the Continental Cablevision Contest and didn't win the first time. But he won the second time! Although he is a principal, he makes time to teach. His video production course was an elective for the students, who videotaped various school events and worked with Sam Price, a freelance television producer who lives in Rollinsford. Sam helped the students learn how to edit the tape. Students self-critiqued their work.

Jay feels teachers need to be taught how to read technical manuals. When he was given a gas grill for Father's Day one year, he wanted to cry. Reading a 50-page manual and assembling dozens of parts hadn't been part of his education while growing up. His students, on the other hand, whether faced with a television, VCR, or video camera manual, are more technologically savvy and have no hesitation about jumping right in.

Jay told me about a veteran teacher in his building, Nan Hodgdon, who uses cable programming. Last year, she used the Discovery Channel series on the solar system and turned her below-ground-level classroom into a spaceship. Her whole year was thematically based on space exploration. Her class started a classroom newspaper called *The Comet Times*. Next year, she is going medieval, complete with castle walls.

> Tip: *If you don't think you are able to use a VCR, ask a kid in the classroom. A student can usually set it up.*

Micheline Woolfolk, Library Media Specialist, John M. Gandy Elementary School, Ashland, Virginia. Using Continental Cablevision's aforementioned *Classroom Guide to Master Control—Television Literacy for Kids*, Micheline's third, fourth, and fifth graders learned critical viewing skills, which culminated in published letters and a video documentary on how to critically view television.

Micheline, the school library media specialist, would love to tell you that she had this wonderful idea, carefully planned this media literacy project for months and months, implemented it, and saw it to fruition. But this wasn't the case at all. The truth is, she says, it just fell into place—evolving as it was happening.

She had 11 students watch the *Master Control* videotape and then use their new critical eyes to write articles on an environmental program of their choice. They submitted all of their articles to *Better Viewing*, a media literacy magazine published by Continental Cablevision, which provides information on viewing television constructively.

When one student's article wasn't published, Micheline's project took another turn. She wanted to provide this student with another publishing opportunity. So she called her friend, Terry Shiels, a producer of *Plight of the Futaleufu*, a thought-provoking 30-minute PBS video debating the future of a free-flowing river located below the Andes mountains. Her students wrote to him, asking technical questions about how the video was filmed and about his personal views. They e-mailed their letters, and he responded to each one.

Micheline got the idea to videotape the children as they watched *Plight*. Afterward, she had the students ask one another questions about what they just watched.

She ended up with a video with a silent beginning. She had to find a way to add sound, so she attended a technology conference and enrolled in a class on television operation. A piecemeal approach, no doubt, but it resulted in an award-winning project nonetheless.

If Micheline could go back in time with her project, she would do one thing differently. At the end of each school year, an award assembly recognizes children for perfect attendance and academic achievement—Micheline now wishes she had asked that an award be given to media-literate students as well.

> Tip: *You don't necessarily have to start a cable project with everything planned. Begin with an idea and run with it.*

Creating an
Information Renaissance

Rachelle B. Chong

It is a great pleasure to be here at this National Educator Awards luncheon sponsored by Continental Cablevision. We are here today to recognize and applaud some of the most innovative teachers, librarians, media specialists, and administrators in America.

These are teachers who have embraced technology. They understand that a multimedia experience can impart a richer learning experience than mere textbooks. They are teachers who wisely use the power of television to pique their students' interests and teach.

I applaud Continental Cablevision for giving these wonderful awards and thereby encouraging these teachers' efforts.

Education in an Information Age

I wanted to talk today about the important role of telecommunications infrastructure and applications in preparing our students for jobs in an increasingly global economy—an economy based on information.

With the astonishing popularity of personal computers and the tremendous advances in communications technology of the last decades, it seems clear that we have truly entered the Information Age.

I'm personally glad that we have moved beyond the Industrial Age. To me, that era was characterized by impersonality and dehumanization.

In contrast, the Information Age promises to be much more enriching—more like the Renaissance, which, if you recall, was a period marked by intellectual activity and the flowering of the arts, literature, and science.

I would like to suggest that we are entering an Information Renaissance, and in this era, there is important work to be done by educators. In an Information Age, students will need to be conversant in a wide variety of communications technologies. It is a fact that our society is increasingly a "high-tech" one. Nowadays, in a typical business office you will find as standard equipment computers, fax machines, and electronic mail. Already, 40% of American households have a personal computer.

Our citizens must have technological savvy to function in this world. But are our educators—those who are shaping our future workers—up to this challenge?

Reed Hundt, the chairman of the Federal Communications Commission (FCC), has said, "There are thousands of buildings in this country, and millions of people in them who have no telephones, no cable television, and no reasonable prospect of broadband services: They are called schools."

Just as students outgrew the use of colonial McGuffey readers, our students are moving beyond the use of the textbooks and chalkboards that were the basic tools when I was in school.

As citizens of one of the most technologically advanced countries of the world, American students deserve state-of-the-art educational facilities and educational tools. This includes telecommunications technology.

You have probably heard a lot of hype about the Information Superhighway. The heart of the concept is that private industries would create a global network of communications and computer networks that will help transmit information quickly and inexpensively across traditional boundaries of time and space.

Some go as far as to suggest that, in the future, countries won't be trading natural resources or products; they'll be trading information. Knowledge will be power.

Besides business applications, the Information Superhighway holds great promise to benefit our educational system. One idea is to create a global digital library containing the best of the world's libraries and museums. For example, you would scan in the Mona Lisa and the Declaration of Independence. Children everywhere could access these historical treasures with the click of a mouse.

In this way, we could literally put the world's cultural riches at every child's desktop. These kinds of ideas make me believe that the renaissance of the 21st century lies in the successful creation of an Information Superhighway.

If we are successful, the Information Superhighway will allow any child—rich or poor—access to information. As many of us know, education is still the great equalizer of our democratic society. We must work to help education keep pace with technological advances, so that it can keep pace with societal needs.

How do we prepare our students for a world in which advanced information technologies will be as commonplace as the computer and fax machine are in today's offices? I wanted to share with you some ideas that I have, and to describe what the FCC is doing in this area.

The big news is that a new law has just been enacted that will help connect the schools to the Information Superhighway. In February, the Telecommunications Act of 1996 was passed. It has two provisions of particular interest to educators.

Section 254(h) of the new act directs the FCC to establish rules to enhance, to the extent technically feasible and economically reasonable, access to advanced telecommunications and information services for all public and nonprofit elementary and secondary school classrooms and libraries.

The law directs telecommunications carriers serving a geographic area to provide communications services for educational purposes to schools and libraries at discounted rates. Further, the law makes clear that those living in rural areas should not be left out, and requires that rates between urban and rural areas be generally comparable.

Section 706(a) of the act instructs the FCC and state commissions to encourage the deployment of advanced telecommunications capability to all Americans, including, in particular, elementary and secondary schools and classrooms.

The commission has started proceedings to implement the new law. We are committed to adopting policies that will encourage the connection of our schools to the outside world for the purpose of education.

This new communications infrastructure may include a variety of options, depending on the needs of the school. It could consist of wired or wireless telephones in every classroom. Just the presence of a phone in a classroom greatly enhances a teacher's safety and effectiveness.

A classroom phone—and features such as voice mail—also brings better and immediate communication between teachers and parents. Students no longer will be able to claim that "the dog ate my homework" because a teacher can pick up the phone to check out the story!

The addition of a phone line, a computer, and a modem to the classroom allows the students to connect with the Internet and explore the world outside the four walls of the classroom.

Making computers available to educators will allow them to communicate with each other on the Internet. Teachers can share innovative lesson plans, while administrators can share technology strategies and applications.

Another possible application could be wired or wireless local area networks that will link students and faculty in a variety of ways. These networks could provide things such as electronic mail, data sharing (say, between a central library and other libraries on campus or even another campus), Internet access, and the like.

Today, the FCC proposed to set aside a large chunk of spectrum for unlicensed broadband wireless devices, capable of high-speed transmissions of multimedia information. One suggested use of these so called NII/SUPERNET devices is to provide wireless broadband networks within buildings and between classrooms. These wireless devices could enable desktop access to the Internet for students, and you wouldn't have to string a tangle of wires around the room or through asbestos-filled walls.

New broadband networks also have the potential to provide distance-learning opportunities. For example, a professor at an urban university could teach rural students from afar.

Training of Personnel

My next suggestion goes to the issue of training personnel to manage this new communications infrastructure. Once the infrastructure is put in place, our schools must be able to maintain and use these communications devices effectively.

Because they set budgets, school administrators will need to study and understand technology trends. They will need to allocate enough money to ensure the infrastructure is put in place and that the equipment is maintained and upgraded as technology advances. Just as a school needs a custodian to maintain its physical facilities, it will need a trained technician to keep the communications and computer facilities working smoothly.

Further, it is very important that teachers, librarians, and media specialists be trained in how to effectively incorporate multimedia tools into curricula. Let's face it. Many adults cannot even figure out how to program their VCRs, much less figure out how to surf the Internet!

We must encourage all educators to overcome any technophobia and become comfortable and hopefully excited about the benefits and efficiencies that technology can bring. As we all know, technology will never replace teachers. But technology is a wonderful tool to help teachers be more effective.

I would encourage educators to put significant efforts into learning how to use technology. The use of information technologies in the classroom is only limited by the imagination of the instructor.

Educational Content

This brings me to my third point. Educational curricula should be adapted to take full advantage of new multimedia techniques. Cable programmers, broadcasters, software developers, and others are developing some wonderful educational material that can be brought into the classroom by educators. As we all know, kids love television, and it can be a terrific teaching tool.

I am pleased that these industries have taken a leadership role in developing quality educational content. I especially commend the cable industry on its outstanding Cable in the Classroom program, and other industry groups for their comparable efforts.

In particular, I salute Amos Hostetter Jr., the chairman and CEO of Continental Cablevision. Continental Cablevision has been an active and committed leader in promoting the use of cable television in the classroom.

A Salute to Teachers

Now, if you've got the infrastructure, the technicians, and the lesson plans, you must still have teachers who understand how to integrate technology into the classroom. So my last point is that to make all this work, you need teachers who are in on the program.

Many of the teachers being honored today have used educational programming from cable providers to great effect. I salute you because it takes courage, creativity, and energy to be a teacher who uses technology as a teaching tool in these times of budget problems, overcrowding, and outdated facilities. You are role models for teachers everywhere.

I am especially proud of Manuel Moreno, a science teacher at my alma mater, Lincoln High School in Stockton, California. His students produced a weekly live cable program on the human body that was beamed—via Continental Cablevision's two-way, interactive television system—from the high school campus to preteen students at Brookside School.

His students worked in teams to choose topics of interest to the younger students, ranging from the skeletal system to acne—a timely topic during adolescence! His students wrote the scripts, acted, and produced the half-hour shows.

During the pilot program, the high school students dissected a cow's eye as the younger students looked on in amazement and, maybe, with some queasiness! I'm sure the show was "udderly moo-tivating!"

To use his words, Mr. Moreno wanted students to realize that "learning is cool" and to recognize the value of hands-on science. He realized that using Cable in the Classroom helped him get the undivided attention of his students. This is one teacher who effectively used technology to reach his students—and, hopefully, to inspire them onward to careers in medicine, science, or teaching.

It is a real inspiration to see teachers such as Manuel Moreno using such imaginative and ingenious ways to reach their students. I believe that each time a teacher gets a student excited about learning, there will be a ripple effect. That is one more student who will be a contributor to our society. It's an old saying, but it's true: From little acorns, mighty oaks will grow.

It will take a partnership of government, industry, and educators to get technology into the classroom. Government can encourage policies that put the infrastructure in place. Industry has stepped up to the plate to voluntarily connect the schools and provide the necessary training and content for teachers. And of course, educators such as today's award winners are using technology to dazzle and inspire their students.

I hope that this partnership can help bring about a new Information Renaissance in the 21st century, one that will again bring us intellectual activity and a new flowering of the arts, literature, and science.

Congratulations to our award-winning teachers, and thanks!

**CORWIN
PRESS**

The Corwin Press logo—a raven striding across an open book—represents the happy union of courage and learning. We are a professional-level publisher of books and journals for K–12 educators, and we are committed to creating and providing resources that embody these qualities. Corwin's motto is "Success for All Learners."

Printed in the United States
By Bookmasters